GREAT WESTERN
4-6-0s

GREAT WESTERN
4-6-0s

LOCOMOTIVES
ILLUSTRATED

BRIAN STEPHENSON

LONDON
IAN ALLAN LTD

First published 1984
Reprinted 1996

ISBN 0 7110 1363 2

© Ian Allan Ltd 1984

Published by Ian Allan Ltd, Shepperton, Surrey;
and printed by Ian Allan Printing Ltd,
Coombelands House, Addlestone, Surrey KT15 1HY

Contents

TITLE PAGE: 'Castle' class 4-6-0 No 7027 *Thornbury Castle* hurries from Box Tunnel with a Paddington-Bristol express on 27 May 1956.
D. M. C. Hepburne-Scott/Rail Archive Stephenson

LEFT: 'Manor' class 4-6-0 No 7814 *Fringford Manor* approaches Paignton with a down goods on 23 July 1957.
D. M. C. Hepburne-Scott/Rail Archive Stephenson

Preface

When *Locomotives Illustrated No 1* made its appearance in 1974, there was no telling that 10 years later the series would still be going strong. Such is the continuing appeal of the steam locomotive that perhaps no one should be surprised at the success of this quarterly production. Those involved with the preparation of *Locomotives Illustrated* have staged the appearance of the locomotive classes so that all the aces — the popular classes — would not be played at once. However, more than one 'family' of classes has now been completed which explains the appearance of this book. Although it includes material from the five issues of *Locomotives Illustrated*, dealing with GWR 4-6-0 locomotives, for reasons connected with production it does not include every photograph featured in the separate magazines. Also for reasons of space, it has not be practicable to reproduce the *Introductions* to each issue, but the f tabular matter is reproduced, updated and corrected as necessary.

The success of *Locomotives Illustrated* owes much to Bri Stephenson, the Picture Editor, who has put in so much work ensure not only that each issue is comprehensive pictorially, but h prepared the tabular matter and looked out the best and mo interesting photographs available. The publishers would like to ta this opportunity to express their thanks.

Michael Harr
Series Edit

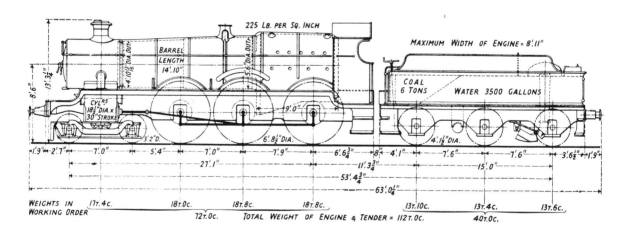

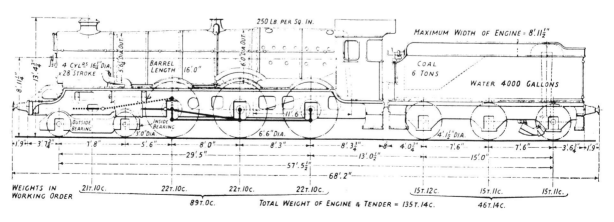

TOP: 'Saint' in latter day condition.

ABOVE: 'King' in as introduced condition.

1 The 'Saints' and 'Stars'

BELOW: In the last year of its life, but largely altered in appearance, 'Star' class 4-6-0 No 4059 *Princess Patricia* climbs towards the summit of Sapperton with the Sunday 11.40am Swindon-Gloucester train on 19 April 1952. *Philip M. Alexander*

TOP: The Great Western Railway's first express passenger 4-6-0 No 100 *William Dean* threads the South Devon cliffs near Dawlish with a Paddington-Plymouth express in the mid-1900s. *L&GRP No 21407, courtesy David & Charles*

ABOVE: Following two further 4-6-0s, Nos 98 and 171 built in 1903, a further batch of 19 engines was turned out in 1905. Of these 13 were built as Atlantics though they were later rebuilt as 4-6-0s. The Atlantics became known as the 'Scotts' and No 186 *Robin Hood* is seen in its original condition. *Ian Allan Library*

UPPER RIGHT: Next followed the 10 'Ladies' built in May 1906. No 2901, the first of these, was famous for being the first locomotive built by and used on a British railway that was equipped with a modern superheater. The remaining nine engines and the 20 'Saints' that followed the 'Ladies' were not superheated at first. No 2902 *Lady of the Lake* is seen arriving at Paddington with an up express about 1908. *Lens of Sutton*

LOWER RIGHT: After the 'Saints' proper came the final series of 25 'Courts'. They were built with superheaters and had the neater curved drop-ends to the framing. No 2934 *Butleigh Court* is in pre-World War 1 condition. The brass beading to the splashers was removed from both the 'Stars' and 'Saints' during that war. *Ian Allan Library*

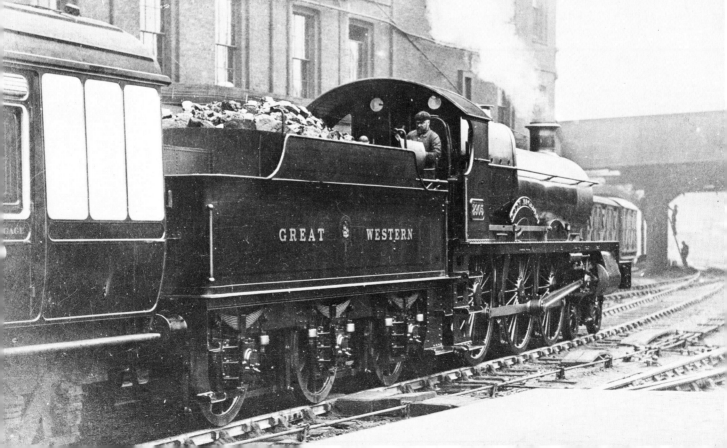

UPPER LEFT: 'Saint' No 2905 *Lady Macbeth* departs from Paddington shortly after Grouping with a down express. *Lens of Sutton*

LOWER LEFT: Another view of No 2905 *Lady Macbeth* awaiting to leave Paddington very early in its life and before the massive Bishops Bridge was built. *Ian Allan Library*

BELOW: Two 'Saints' were fairly extensively rebuilt in later years. No 2925 *Saint Martin* was modified in 1924 to be the prototype of the 'Hall' class and No 2935 *Caynham Court*, as seen here, was rebuilt in May 1931 with rotary cam poppet valve gear and new cylinders. *LPC/Ian Allan Library*

BOTTOM: The 13 Atlantics with names having associations with Sir Walter Scott were rebuilt as 4-6-0s in 1912/13. As seen in this picture No 2980 *Coeur de Lion* heading a down train of milk empties to Ealing Broadway they received curved frame drop-ends, thus bringing them into line with the 'Saints' and 'Courts'. *Lens of Sutton*

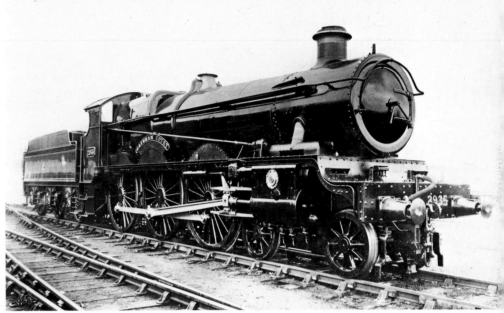

ABOVE: The third 4-6-0 to be built in what became the 'Saint' class, No 2971 *Albion*, awaits its next duty at Swindon shed in the mid-1930s. This engine ran as an Atlantic between October 1903 and July 1907 to compare with the French 4-4-2s. It retains its original nameplate without the raised backing plate. *Lens of Sutton*

BELOW: In its final form with outside steam pipes, No 2920 *Saint David*, destined to be the last survivor of its class, stands beside the turntable at Chester on 4 September 1937. *T. G. Hepburn/Rail Archive Stephenson*

UPPER RIGHT: No 40 near Acton with a down express from Paddington while still running as an Atlantic. It was renumbered 4000 in December 1912. *LPC/Ian Allan Library*

CENTRE RIGHT: 'Star' No 4005 *Polar Star* passes Kilburn & Maida Vale station with a Euston-Liverpool express on 27 August 1910 during the GWR/LNWR locomotive exchange. *H. Gordon Tidey/Ian Allan Library*

BELOW: Another picture of *Polar Star* on the LNWR, seen departing from Euston with a down express during the 1910 exchange. The locomotive sent to the GWR was 'Experiment' 4-6-0 No 1471 *Worcestershire*. *Ian Allan Library*

ABOVE: Following the first batch of 'Stars' came Nos 4011-20, named after Knights and followed by 10 Kings which had much more graceful curved framing over the inside cylinders. The first of this batch, No 4021, was superheated from new but the remainder were superheated at a later date though all engines from No 4031 had it from new. Here No 4026 *King Richard* departs from Paddington with the 4.38pm boat express for Fishguard Harbour connecting with the *ss Lusitania* bound for New York on 21 August 1910. With the introduction of Collett's 'Kings' from 1927 all the 'Star' class Kings were renamed Monarchs with No 4026 becoming *Japanese Monarch*. Not surprisingly this name was removed in 1941.
CGB Ken Nunn Collection

RIGHT: Star No 4027 *King Henry* awaits departure from Paddington about 1910. This engine became *Norwegian Monarch* in 1927.
Ian Allan Library

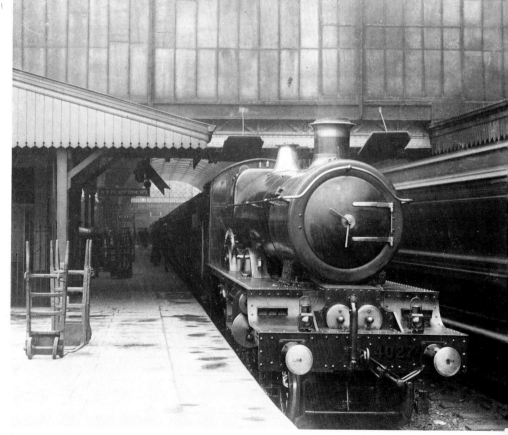

UPPER LEFT: 'Star' No 4038 *Queen Berengaria* passes Twyford East Box with a down express from Paddington in the late 1920s. *Lens of Sutton*

LOWER LEFT: 'Star' No 4012 *Knight of the Thistle* makes a rare appearance on a goods train in about 1930 and is seen having just passed Teignmouth in the up direction. *Lens of Sutton*

BELOW: No 4024 *Dutch Monarch* takes water from Ruislip troughs with an up Birmingham line express in the late 1920s. *LPC/Ian Allan Library*

BOTTOM: No 4057 *Princess Elizabeth* leans to the curve at Skewen with the 8.55am Paddington-Swansea express in about 1929. *F. R. Hebron/Rail Archive Stephenson*

...in 1939. The engine is fitted with 'elbow' pattern outside steam pipes. These were fitted to some of the class from 1927 when new inside cylinders were fitted in conjunction with the original type outside cylinders. *C. R. L. Coles*

BELOW: Another 'Star' fitted with 'elbow' steam pipes. No 4018 *Knight of the Grand Cross*, has its fire cleaned on Old Oak Common shed in the mid-1930s. Like No 4014, this locomotive was by now superheated and carrying the short type of safety valve bonnet. *Rail Archive Stephenson*

UPPER LEFT: 'Saint' No 2942 *Fawley Court* enters Bristol Temple Meads with a Portsmouth train formed of SR stock in 1938. *C. R. L. Coles*

LOWER LEFT: An up West of England express passes Taplow in 1938 hauled by No 2903 *Lady of Lyons*. This was the first of the 'Saints' to receive outside steam pipes in November 1930. These indicated a complete renewal of the front end of the locomotive which in the case of No 2903 also included a curved drop to the framing although retaining the straight rear end. Note the leading non-corridor coach. *C. R. L. Coles*

BELOW: Now renumbered 2900, the pioneer 'Saint', *William Dean*, approaches Reading with an up express in the mid-1920s. It was withdrawn in 1932 when its non-standard cylinders had worn out. *M. W. Earley*

BOTTOM: Former Atlantic No 2980 *Coeur de Lion* nears Iver with the 3.55pm Paddington-South Wales express in 1935. *F. R. Hebron/Rail Archive Stephenson*

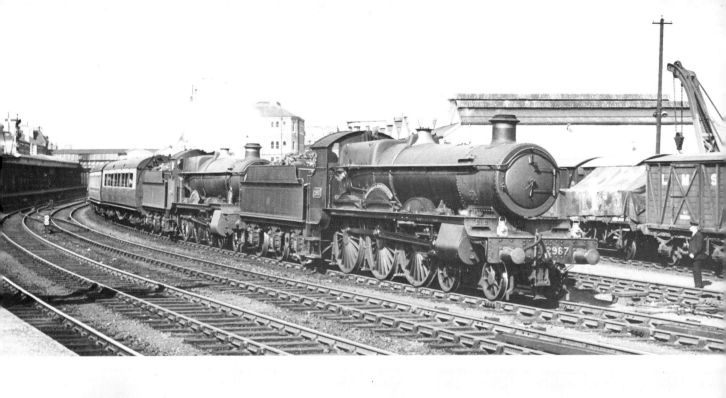

UPPER LEFT: No 2912 *Saint Ambrose* heads a Paddington-Bristol semi-fast through Sonning cutting 1939. *M. W. Earley*

LOWER LEFT: Now coupled to a Collett tender, No 2916 *Saint Benedict* pulls away from Slough with an up train in 1938 as a '61xx' 2-6-2T heads a down suburban train into the station. *R. L. Coles*

TOP: Another former Atlantic, No 2987 *Bride of Lammermoor*, pilots a 'Grange' 4-6-0 out of Newport the late 1930s. *Rail Archive Stephenson*

ABOVE: No 2902 *Lady of the Lake* sets out from Westbury with a local train in the late 1930s. *Ian Allan Library*

BELOW: 'Star' No 4062 *Malmesbury Abbey* passes Flax Bourton with an up West of England expre[ss] in 1939. The engine is coupled to a Collett 4,000-gallon tender. *C. R. L. Coles*

RIGHT: A down Birmingham line express passes West Ruislip headed by 'Star' No 4023 *Danish Monarch* in the late 1920s. *LPC/Ian Allan Library*

LEFT: 'Star' No 4004 *Morning Star* on arrival at Nottingham Victoria in the late 1930s with a train from the SR via Banbury which it had taken over at Oxford. *T. G. Hepburn/Rail Archive Stephenson*

BOVE: No 4022 *Belgian Monarch* pulls out of Taunton with an up West of England train in 1937. *R. L. Coles*

ABOVE: 'Star' No 4038 *Queen Berengaria* **waits to leave Paddington with a down express in 1938.** *L. Hanson*

UPPER RIGHT: No 4007 *Rising Star* **waits for departure time at Paddington early in 1937. Later th** year the engine was renamed *Swallowfield Park*. *E. E. Smith*

LOWER RIGHT: On the same night in 1937 No 4019 *Knight Templar* **waits at Paddington with a** down express. *E. E. Smith*

FAR LEFT ABOVE: 'Star' No 4013 *Knight of St Patrick* heads out of Chester with a Birkenhead-Ruabon train in the late 1940s. *Eric Treacy*

FAR LEFT BELOW: No 4043 *Prince Henry* near Dawlish Warren with the 10am Sunday Paignton-Newcastle express on 5 June 1949. The engine has 'Castle' type outside steam pipes indicating the fitting of new pattern outside cylinders. *E. D. Bruton*

LEFT: In BR livery 'Saint' No 2927 *Saint Patrick* enters Chippenham with a Taunton-Paddington train on 24 March 1951. *G. J. Jefferson*

BELOW: 'Star' No 4060 *Princess Eugenie* rounds the curve out of Sydney Gardens as it leaves Bath with a Bristol-Weymouth train in July 1951. *Derek Cross*

UPPER LEFT: Double-headed 'Saints' were very rare but it must have been even rarer to find Nos 2920 *Saint David* and 2937 *Clevedon Court* climbing the Lickey Incline assisted by the 0-10-0 banker No 58100 on an 11-coach northbound express on Saturday, 16 September 1950. *R. Hewitt*

CENTRE LEFT: One of the 'Ladies' with renewed front-ends, No 2906 *Lady of Lynn*, stands in Cardiff General during August 1951. *P. Ransome-Wallis*

BELOW: Another view of No 2937 *Clevedon Court* now freshly painted in BR lined black livery. *Ian Allan Library*

UPPER RIGHT: The 11.55pm Saturday night Manchester-Plymouth train enters Teignmouth hauled by No 2979 *Quentin Durward* — the last survivor of the 'Saints' rebuilt from Atlantics. *E. D. Bruton*

LOWER RIGHT: No 2931 *Arlington Court* has just coupled to a Brighton-Cardiff train at Salisbury on 18 February 1950. *W. Gilburt*

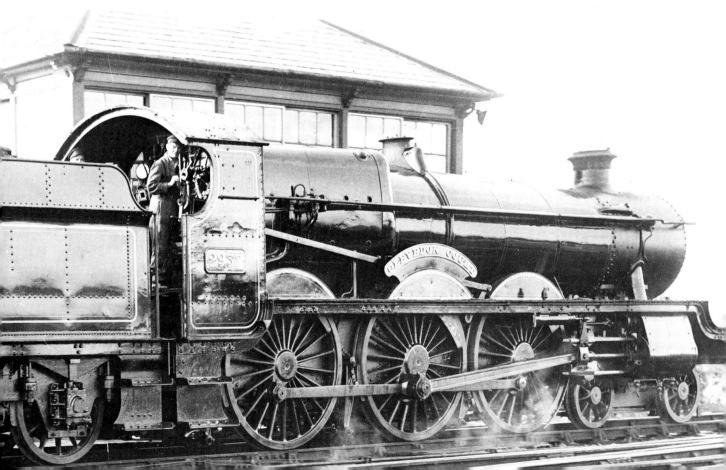

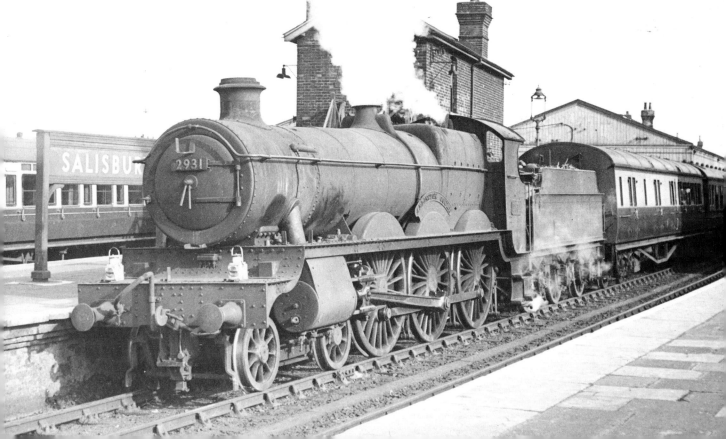

BELOW: 'Star' No 4056 *Princess Margaret* climbs away from Kingswear with a local for Exeter on 3 December 1955. This was to be the last 'Star' to remain in traffic.   *D. S. Fish*

BOTTOM: No 4042 *Prince Albert* is reduced to hauling a 'B' set forming the 5.32pm local train to Weston-super-Mare, departing Bristol Temple Meads in September 1951.   *J. D. Mills*

2 The 'Castles'

ABOVE: The 3.30pm Paddington-Plymouth express approaches West Drayton behind No 4082 *Windsor Castle* on 23 July 1926. For some reason this engine has been sent out with its safety valve bonnet missing; a most unusual occurrence. *F. R. Hebron/Rail Archive Stephenson*

LEFT: No 4097 *Kenilworth Castle* was only one month old when this picture was taken of it passing West Drayton on 23 July 1926, with a Bristol-Paddington train formed more of vans than passenger coaches.
F. R. Hebron/Rail Archive Stephenson

RIGHT: No 4079 *Pendennis Castle* has acquired an intermediate-type tender in place of its original 3,500-gallon type in this photograph taken at Old Oak Common about 1935.
Rail Archive Stephenson

BELOW: A Swansea-Paddington express passes under the Skewen arches hauled by No 4076 *Carmarthen Castle* about 1929. This engine has the standard 4,000-gallon tender introduced in 1926.
F. R. Hebron/Rail Archive Stephenson

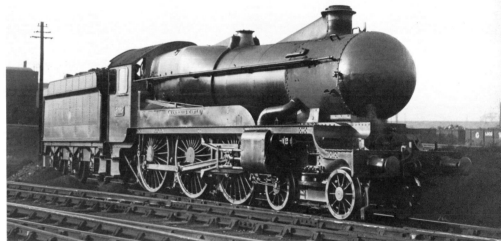

UPPER LEFT: No 4079 *Pendennis Castle* **will always be remembered for its part in the GWR-LNER locomotive exchange of 1925 when it took the wind out of the LNER sails during the week of 27 April- 2 May 1925. In this view we see** *Pendennis Castle* **departing from King's Cross the previous week with the 10.12am slow train to Peterborough while its crew were learning the route.**

LOWER LEFT: During the actual trials No 4079 *Pendennis Castle* **departs from King's Cross with the 1.30pm express to Leeds, which it worked through to Doncaster on 28 April 1925. No 4079 regularly lifted its 475-ton trains past Finsbury Park in under six minutes and usually arrived at Peterborough and Doncaster well before time. The lesson learnt from the trial was put to good use by the LNER and it was not many years before their Pacifics had reversed the position.**

TOP: Another 'Castle' to run on LNER metals in 1925 was No 4082 *Windsor Castle***, which in company with No 111** *Viscount Churchill* **took part in the Stockton & Darlington Railway Centenary celebrations. Here No 4082 heads the GWR Royal Train in the procession on 2 July 1925, while No 111 had charge of a train of new articulated stock.** *Windsor Castle* **was very much the GWR royal engine, for it was driven from Swindon Works to the station by King George V on 28 April 1924, and carried a commemorative brass plate on the cabside. It was later to haul the King's funeral train to Windsor on 28 January 1936. It was to have performed the same sad duty for King George VI on 13 February 1952, but was not available so its name and number were exchanged with No 7013** *Bristol Castle* **and it never reverted to its old identity.**
All: F. R. Hebron/Rail Archive Stephenson

ABOVE: In March 1935 No 5005 *Manorbier Castle* **was partially streamlined on somewhat similar lines to the windcutters of the Paris, Lyons & Mediterranean Railway. This illustration shows No 5005 at Old Oak Common on 12 October 1935, with the casing which enveloped the cylinders, steam pipes and steam chests already removed.**
K. A. C. R. Nunn/LCGB Ken Nunn Collection

ABOVE: No **5007** *Rougemont Castle* steams over Exminster water troughs with the down Torbay Express c1930. *F. R. Hebron/Rail Archive Stephenson*

BELOW: Even when at rest in Old Oak Common shed when still quite new No 4080 *Powderham Castle* is a study of power and elegance. *Lens of Sutton*

UPPER LEFT: One of the 15 'Castles' rebuilt from 'Star' Class 4-6-0s No 100 A1 *Lloyd's* climbs the 1 in 98 up to Bruton with a 14-coach Plymouth-Paddington express in the late 1930s. Note the bogie brakevan next to the engine inscribed Ocean Mails. This engine was originally No 4009 *Shooting Star* built in 1907 and was rebuilt as a 'Castle' in 1925. It was renumbered and renamed 100 A1 *Lloyd's* in 1936 but it cannot have been a very good risk for it was the first 'Castle' to be withdrawn about five months before the last engine of the class was completed at Swindon in 1950. *Ian Allan Library*

LOWER LEFT: The partially streamlined No 5005 *Manorbier Castle* approaches Westbourne Park with an up express from Taunton on 14 July 1937. The bullnose and cowlings behind the chimney and safety valves were removed in 1943 and the wedge-shaped cab was replaced in 1947. *John P. Wilson*

BELOW: An unidentified 'Castle' hurries a down Taunton express through Sonning cutting in the late 1930s. *M. W. Earley*

RIGHT: No 4081 *Warwick Castle* threads its way beneath the bridges at Teignmouth station with the Saturday-only 8.35am Falmouth-Paddington express on 11 June 1949. *E. D. Bruton*

FAR RIGHT: No 5086 *Viscount Horne* pulls into Bristol Temple Meads with a Penzance and Kingswear-Wolverhampton express on 4 June 1949. The 10 'Castles' Nos 5083-92 were rebuilt from 'Star' class engines Nos 4063-72. *John P. Wilson*

LOWER RIGHT: With a liberal coating of postwar grime, No 5058 *Earl of Clancarty* heads the down Torbay Express along the South Devon coast between Dawlish and Teignmouth on 5 June 1949. *John P. Wilson*

BELOW: No 4089 *Donnington Castle* blasts out of Parsons Rock Tunnel between Dawlish and Teignmouth with a down express in the mid 1950s. *T. G. Hepburn/Rail Archive Stephenson*

BELOW: No 5097 *Sarum Castle* pulls away from Dawlish with an up train in the early 1950s. It is coupled with a straight-sided Hawksworth tender. *T. G. Hepburn/Rail Archive Stephenson*

BOTTOM: On a running-in turn from Swindon works No 4097 *Kenilworth Castle* nears Uffington with a Didcot-Swindon local on 6 October 1951. *J. F. Russell-Smith*

RIGHT: No 5094 *Tretower Castle* raises the echoes under an azure sky as it storms the steepest part of the climb to Sapperton Tunnel, the 1 in 60 near Frampton Crossing on 13 October 1956, with the 11.30am Cheltenham-Paddington express. *George Heiron*

UPPER LEFT: No 111 *Viscount Churchill* heads a Sunday Plymouth-Paddington train near Uphill Junction, Weston-super-Mare, on 13 April 1952. This engine was a rebuild of the Churchward Pacific No 111 *The Great Bear*. *J. D. Mills*

LOWER LEFT: The up 'Torbay Express' from Kingswear to Paddington approaches Dawlish hauled by one of the postwar 'Castles', No 7001 *Sir James Milne*, in the early 1950s. *T. G. Hepburn/Rail Archive Stephenson*

RIGHT: The 4.08pm train for Paddington via Oxford awaits departure time at Birmingham Snow Hill with No 5029 *Nunney Castle* in charge on 8 February 1958. *M. Mensing*

BELOW: No 5033 *Broughton Castle* has just crossed the River Thames between Culham and Radley with a down express in the late afternoon of 26 November 1955. *D. M. C. Hepburne-Scott/Rail Archive Stephenson*

RIGHT: A Kingwear-Bristol excursion train climbs the 1 in 66 over the Maypool Viaduct on the approach to Greenway Tunnel behind No 5053 *Earl Cairns* on 8 September 1957. The Earl names were originally intended for the '32xx' class 4-4-0s, better known as 'Dukedogs', but only 12 received them before it was decided to put the names on to 'Castle' class engines. *D. S. Fish*

BELOW: No 7001 *Sir James Milne* heads east into the gathering dusk at Badminton with a South Wales-Paddington express on 20 February

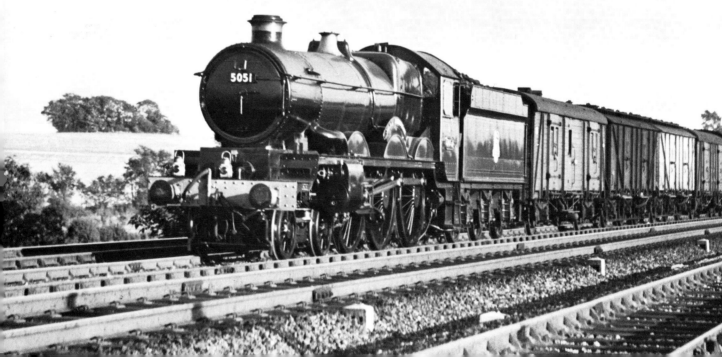

UPPER LEFT: No 5067 *St Fagans Castle* heads an up South Wales express near Pangbourne on 11 May 1955. *D. M. C. Hepburne-Scott/Rail Archive Stephenson*

LOWER LEFT: In sparkling ex-works condition No 5051 *Earl Bathurst* approaches Didcot with a down parcels train on 9 October 1955. *D. M. C. Hepburne-Scott/Rail Archive Stephenson*

TOP: No 5015 *Kingswear Castle* speeds down the gradient from Saunderton summit into Princes Risborough with the 4.10pm Paddington-Birkenhead express on 31 May 1951. *J. C. Flemons*

ABOVE: The up 'Cathedrals Express' is seen near Yarnton, north of Oxford, hauled by No 5042 *Winchester Castle* on 20 October 1959. *D. M. C. Hepburne-Scott/Rail Archive Stephenson*

UPPER LEFT: No 5031 *Totnes Castle* threads the Chilterns as it approaches Saunderton summit with the 4.10pm Paddington-Birkenhead express on 28 August 1952. *J. F. Russell-Smith*

LOWER LEFT: No 7025 *Sudeley Castle* passes Twyford with the up 'Welsh Dragon' in the early 1950s. *M. W. Earley*

ABOVE: In 1956 No 7018 *Drysllwyn Castle* was fitted with an experimental double chimney and is seen here approaching Churston on test with a dynamometer car at the head of the up 'Torbay Express' on 27 July 1956. This engine at the time had a three-row superheater boiler but from April 1957 double chimneys were fitted to all engines that received four-row superheaters. *D. S. Fish*

RIGHT: No 7014 *Caerhays Castle*, fitted with four-row superheater and double chimney, waits to leave Bristol Temple Meads with the up 'Bristolian' on 3 April 1959. *J. R. Smith*

UPPER LEFT: No 5050 *Earl of St Germans*
brings a Birmingham-Birkenhead train into
Wrexham General on 27 September 1958.
Lewis

LOWER LEFT: Gleaming No 7007 *Great
Western* heads out of Paddington with the down
'Cathedrals Express' in July 1961.
J. Blenkinsop

RIGHT: No 7028 *Cadbury Castle* heads the
down 'Pembroke Coast Express' near Wantage
Road on 10 December 1955.
*M. C. Hepburne-Scott/
Rail Archive Stephenson*

BELOW: The pioneer 'Castle' No 4073
Caerphilly Castle is seen near the end of its active
career on arrival at Paddington with the 8.15am
Saturday-only train from Abertillery on 27 March
1959. *Brian Stephenson*

ABOVE: The last regular express turns for 'Castles' were on the Worcester line. Here No 7003 *Elmley Castle* attacks the 1 in 100 of Chipping Campden bank with the 1.10pm Worcester-Paddington train on 2 March 1963. *G. Smith*

RIGHT: Destined to be the last 'Castle' in BR service, No 7029 *Clun Castle* passes West Wycombe with the last regular steam turn from Paddington, the 4.15pm to Banbury on 18 May 1965. *D. M. C. Hepburne-Scott/ Rail Archive Stephenson*

BELOW: The final engine of the class, 'King' 4-6-0 No 6029 *King Edward VIII*, leaves Parsons Rock Tunnel with a Paddington-Plymouth express in the mid 1950s.
T. G. Hepburn/Rail Archive Stephenson

3 The 'Kings'

BELOW: No 6000 *King George V* stands in Paddington station when new. The engine is fitted with a Westinghouse brake pump in readiness for its visit to the USA where it attended the Centenary celebrations of the Baltimore & Ohio Railroad from 24 September-15 October 1927. At the celebrations No 6000 was presented with an American locomotive bell which it has carried to this day. *Lens of Sutton*

RIGHT: No 6014 *King Henry VII* passes Taunton with the up 'Torbay Limited' from Kingswear to Paddington about 1930. This engine was partially streamlined in 1935. *F. R. Hebron/Rail Archive Stephenson*

LOWER RIGHT: No 6013 *King Henry VIII* passes 'Castle' class 4-6-0 No 4080 *Powderham Castle* waiting with an ECS train at the end of the four track section at Norton Fitzwarren as it heads west into the sun with the 1.30pm Paddington-Penzance express about 1930. It was at this point that No 6028 *King George VI* came to grief in November 1940 when it ran through the trap points at the end of the relief line with the 9.50pm Paddington-Penzance sleeping car express just as another 'King' drew clear on the main line with a newspaper train — having the narrowest escape from disaster ever recorded in Britain. The driver of No 6028 had mistaken which line he was on. *F. R. Hebron/Rail Archive Stephenson*

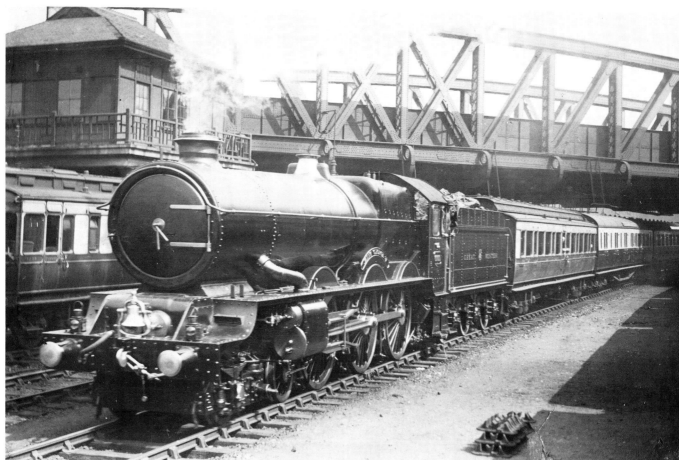

TOP: No 6010 *King Charles I* heads the up 'Torbay Limited' near Burlescombe on 26 August 1929
GWR/Ian Allan Library

ABOVE: No 6000 *King George V*, now fitted with its American bell, departs from Paddington with a
down express in the late 1920s. *Ian Allan Library*

UPPER RIGHT: An afternoon Paddington-Birkenhead express passes West Ruislip hauled by
No 6019 *King Henry V* about 1930. *Ian Allan Library*

LOWER RIGHT: No 6022 *King Edward III* passes Tigley signalbox on the ascent of Rattery bank
with the 3.30pm Paddington-Truro express in June 1939. *H. K. Harman*

LEFT: No 6008 *King James II* passes Northolt
Junction with a down empty stock train on
April 1934.
R. Wethersett/Real Photographs Company

RIGHT: The short lived 'Torquay Pullman'
passes Ruscombe signalbox hauled by No 6004
King George III in 1929. *D. L. Rumble*

BELOW: The up 'Cornish Riviera Express'
passes through Sonning cutting behind No 6012
King Edward VI in the late 1930s. *M. W. Earley*

LEFT: No 6018 *King Henry VI* approaches
Taunton with the up 'Torbay Express' about
1930.
R. Hebron/Rail Archive Stephenson

RIGHT: In March 1935 No 6014 *King Henry
VII* was partially streamlined in the same manner
as 'Castle' class 4-6-0 No 5005 *Manorbier Castle*.
Most of the casing was soon removed from both
engines but No 6014 retained its wedge-shaped
cab to the end. *Ian Allan Library*

BELOW: During the 1948 Locomotive Exchanges No 6018 *King Henry VI* blasts out of Wood Gr[e]
Tunnel with the 1.10pm King's Cross-Leeds and Bradford express on 20 May 1948.
F. R. Hebron/Rail Archive Stephenson

ABOVE: No 6010 *King Charles I* passes Reading shed as it comes round the curve from West to General stations with an up express from Plymouth in final GWR days. *M. W. Earley*

BELOW: No 6022 *King Edward III* accelerates past Reading West with the down 'Cornish Riviera Express' in early BR days. *M. W. Earley*

ABOVE: Beneath an azure sky No 6002 *King William IV* leaves Box Middle Hill Tunnel with the 1.50pm Bristol-Paddington express on 9 October 1954. *George Heiron*

BELOW: The evening sunlight catches No 6025 *King Henry III* as it passes through Dawlish with an up West of England express in September 1955. *P. Ransome-Wallis*

BELOW: 'Hall' class 4-6-0 No 6923 *Croxteth Hall* storms away from an out of course stop at Heathcote Junction signalbox with the 10.08am York-Bournemouth train on 16 May 1964.
Brian Stephenson

4 The 'Halls', 'Granges' and 'Manors'

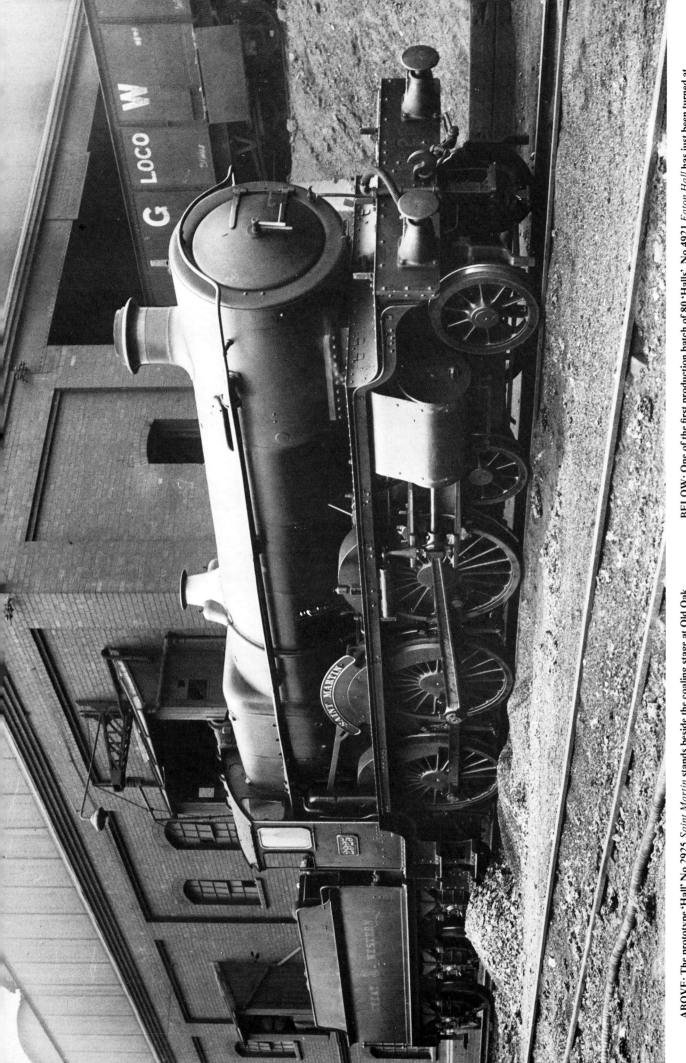

ABOVE: The prototype 'Hall' No 2925 *Saint Martin* stands beside the coaling stage at Old Oak Common in July 1926. It had been rebuilt in 1924 from the 'Saint' class engine originally built in 1907 of the same name and number. The rebuilding consisted of replacing the 6ft 8½in driving wheels with ones of 6ft and fitting a modern side window cab. It was renumbered 4900 in December 1928.

BELOW: One of the first production batch of 80 'Halls', No 4921 *Eaton Hall* has just been turned at the north end of Nottingham Victoria station after working through with an excursion from the South Coast on 17 June 1934. Note the higher pitch of the boiler by 4½in and smaller bogie wheels. Churchward style tenders of 3,500-gallon capacity were fitted to the first 40 or so engines.

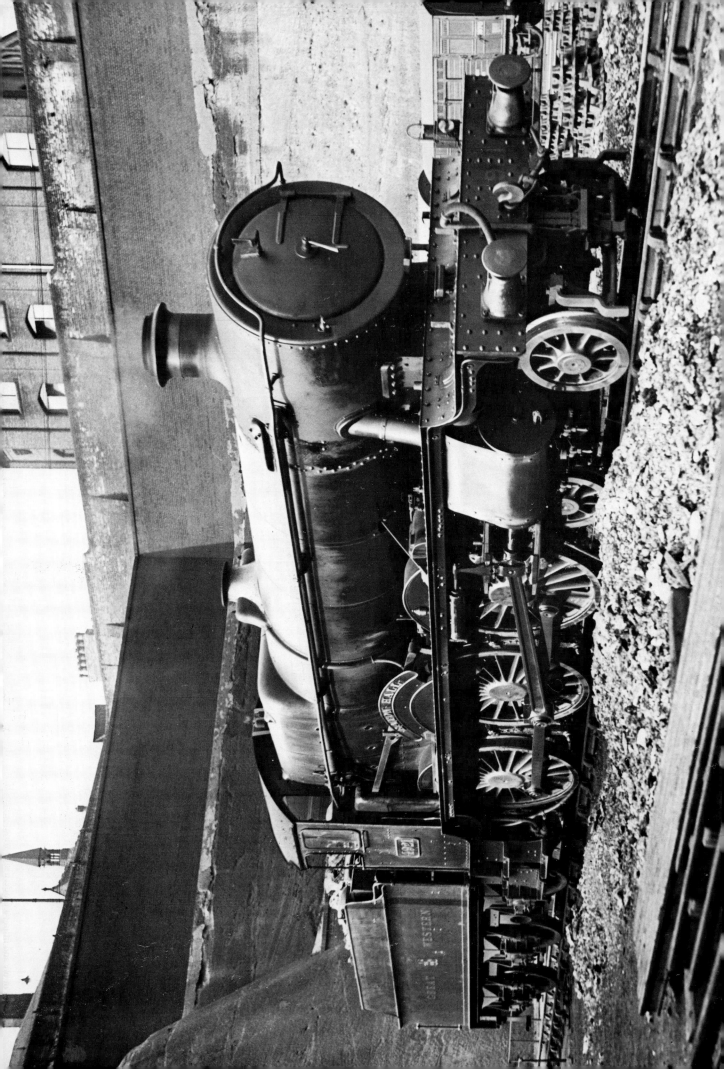

ABOVE: 'Hall' No 5973 *Rolleston Hall,* fitted with the standard Collett 4,000-gallon tender, pulls out of Nottingham Victoria bound for New Basford carriage sidings with the empty stock of an excursion from the SR. *T. G. Hepburn/Rail Archive Stephenson*

RIGHT: No 5973 *Rolleston Hall* is seen again at Nottingham Victoria waiting to depart on the return journey of an excursion from Bournemouth, 30 May 1937. *John P. Wilson*

80

FT: When still quite new, 'Hall' No 4906 *Bradfield Hall* departs from Torquay with an up stopping
m. *Ian Allan Library*

LOW: Fitted with a Collett 3,500-gallon tender, 'Hall' No 4954 *Plaish Hall* departs from
dington with a down semi-fast in the early 1930s. *Lens of Sutton*

UPPER LEFT: The year 1936 saw the introduction of Collett's 'Grange' class 4-6-0. was a smaller wheeled version of the 'Hall'. T incorporated the 5ft 8in wheels and motion of withdrawn Churchward '43xx' series Moguls. Here No 6854 *Roundhill Grange* is being cou to the 11.24am Sheffield-Poole train at Banbu on 22 July 1939. *Ian Allan Library*

CENTRE LEFT: The final 4-6-0 design by Collett was the 'Manor' class, effectively a 'Grange' with a smaller boiler to give a higher route availability, being in the blue category unlike the 'Halls' and 'Granges' which were in red category. Twenty 'Manors' were built in 1938-9 using wheels and motion from withdra '43xx' Moguls while a further 10 completely n engines were built by BR in 1950. Here No 78 *Dunley Manor* waits at Banbury on 22 July 1 with the 8.15am Swansea-Newcastle, a train f which the 'Manors' were purpose-built seeing it ran via the King's Sutton-Kingham-Chelten line. *Ian Allan Library*

RIGHT: 'Grange' No 6854 *Roundhill Grange* seen again as it heads an up freight between S Green and Beaconsfield in 1947. In all 80 'Granges' were built in 1936-9. *E. E. Smith*

LEFT: The first of Hawksworth's 'Modified Hall' class 4-6-0s, No 6959, later to be named *Peatling Hall*, is seen after completion at Swindon in 1944 painted in the wartime plain black livery and without cabside windows. Most of the 'Halls', 'Granges' and 'Manors' had their cabside windows plated over during the war and 'Halls' Nos 6916-70 were not given their nameplates until 1946-8. In all, 71 'Modified Halls' were built during 1944-50 bringing the total number of 'Halls' to 330. The main difference between these and the earlier engines was the use of plate frames throughout, new pattern cylinders and smokebox saddle and a higher degree of superheat.

ABOVE: In 1946/7 11 'Halls' were converted to burn oil and the first so equipped. No 5955 *Garth Hall*, is seen immediately after conversion. It was later renumbered 3950 and all were converted back to coal firing by April 1950. *Both: GWR/Ian Allan Library*

85

PER LEFT: 'Modified Hall' No 7904 *Fountains Hall* approaches South Brent with a Plymouth-ddington express on 21 April 1956. Many of the 'Modified Halls' were given improved draughting ch necessitated a change of chimney. This was a slimmer chimney with no capuchon. Some of these ers later turned up on earlier engines but all could be indentified by the letters ID painted on the t end behind the buffer beam. *D. S. Fish*

WER LEFT: 'Modified Hall' No 7901 *Dodington Hall* has the assistance of '51xx' 2-6-2T No 5113 the climb over Dainton with a parcels train for Plymouth seen leaving Newton Abbot on 13 August 5. *T. E. Williams*

LOW: 'Hall' No 5964 *Wolseley Hall* climbs Dainton with an Exeter-Plymouth stopping train on August 1954. *D. S. Fish*

[UP]PER LEFT: The 'Grange' 4-6-0s did much [work]ling work in the West Country; their smaller [dri]ving wheels being well suited to the many steep [inc]lines. Here No 6873 *Caradoc Grange* passes [Keys?]ra Junction on 30 August 1961 with a down [frei]ght. *R. C. Riley*

[LO]WER LEFT: No 6809 *Burghclere Grange* [climbs?] the bank between Lostwithiel and Bodmin [Ro]ad with an up Class 'H' freight on 25 June [19]55. *R. E. Vincent*

[RI]GHT: The 11.15am Plymouth-Taunton local [asc]ends Hemerdon bank behind No 6836 [Este]varney Grange on 6 August 1956. This [eng]ine carries a boiler with improved draughting [sim]ilar to the 'Modified Halls' previously [me]ntioned. *T. E. Williams*

[BE]LOW: The fireman of No 6817 *Gwenddwr [Gr]ange* collects the token for the passage of the [sin]gle line over the Royal Albert Bridge with a [Ply]mouth-Penzance stopping train in August [19]52. *B. A. Butt*

LEFT: The peace of the Devon countryside is shattered by the sound of 'Hall' No 5904 *Kelham Hall* slogging up Rattery bank from Totnes with an Avonmouth-Tavistock Junction express freight on 28 March 1959. *D. S. Fish*

ABOVE: No 5967 *Bickmarsh Hall* tackles the climb from Princes Risborough to Saunderton with an up loose-coupled freight on 2 February 1954. *J. F. Russell-Smith*

UPPER LEFT: The three great inclines of South Devon — Dainton, Hemerdon and Rattery — led to a lot of double heading when medium power locomotives such as 'Halls' were rostered for heavy trains. Here a pair of 'Halls', Nos 5920 *Wycliffe Hall* and 4908 *Broome Hall*, leave the tunnel at Dainton summit with the 1.45pm Bristol-Newquay train on 29 June 1957. *R. C. Riley*

LOWER LEFT: 'Hall' and 'Modified Hall' Nos 4905 *Barton Hall* and 7903 *Foremarke Hall* are about to descend Hemerdon incline with a Plymouth express on 31 March 1961. *J. C. Beckett*

TOP: 'Halls' Nos 6946 *Heatherden Hall* and 4958 *Priory Hall* bring the 11.15am Newquay-Wolverhampton train into Newton Abbot on 13 August 1961. *W. L. Underhay*

ABOVE: 'Modified Hall' No 7916 *Mobberley Hall* and an unidentified 'Hall' approach Aller Junction with an up Falmouth-Paddington train in September 1959. *Derek Cross*

FT: 'Hall' No 5907 *Marble Hall* hurries past
gbourne with the up 'Cheltenham Spa
ress', the 8am Cheltenham-Paddington on
August 1956.

WER LEFT: Later on the same day a
thbound troop train formed of a mixture of
IS and GW stock approaches Reading West
ind No 6937 *Conyngham Hall*.
h: D. M. C. Hepburne-Scott/
l Archive Stephenson

GHT: The 11.12am Weymouth-Paddington
n passes Wolfhall Junction behind 'Modified
I' No 7924 *Thornycroft Hall* in the mid
0s. *Ivo Peters*

LOW: 'Hall' No 5997 *Sparkford Hall* climbs
ay from Weymouth towards Radipole Halt
h the 4.10pm Weymouth-Paddington train in
tember 1957.
G. Hepburn/Rail Archive Stephenson

94

Newton Hall having just drawn to a stand with a Paddington-Bristol train.

BELOW: Night at Bristol Temple Meads with the 8.43pm local to Swindon waiting to leave behind 'Hall' No 4948 *Northwick Hall. Both: George Heiron*

ABOVE: 'Hall' No 5927 *Guild Hall* **waits to leave Shrewsbury with the 12.10pm Chester-Birmingham relief train on 16 May 1959.** *S. D. Wainwright*

UPPER RIGHT: 'Grange' No 6858 *Woolston Grange* **makes a smoky passage of Whitchurch with an afternoon Manchester-Plymouth train on 3 April 1963.** *M. C. Burge*

LOWER RIGHT: A northbound parcels train rattles over the junction at Craven Arms hauled by 'Modified Hall' No 7920 *Coney Hall* **in June 1964.** *Derek Cross*

TOP: 'Manor' No 7817 *Garsington Manor* comes round the curve off Barmouth Bridge with a Chester–Barmouth train on 11 August 1960. *Derek Cross*

ABOVE: An Aberystwyth train departs from Shrewsbury in the charge of No 7827 *Lydham Manor* on 17 August 1964. *Derek Cross*

UPPER RIGHT: No 7819 *Hinton Manor* climbs past Commins Coch with the up 'Cambrian Coast Express' from Aberystwyth on 4 June 1964. *Derek Cross*

LOWER RIGHT: In happier days when the Western Region still had control of the Cambrian line, gleaming 'Manor' No 7802 *Bradley Manor* comes downhill near Commins Coch Halt with the down 'Cambrian Coast Express' on 16 May 1957. *D. S. Fish*

ABOVE: Shorn of its nameplates 'Manor'
No 7816 *Frilsham Manor* approaches
Micheldever with a northbound parcels train from
Southampton on 20 May 1965.
D. M. C. Hepburne-Scott/
Rail Archive Stephenson

BELOW: On the last day of scheduled steam
working over the SR Redhill-Reading line,
'Manor' No 7829 *Ramsbury Manor*, the last
Great Western designed 4-6-0 to be built, is going
well as it climbs away from Dorking Town with
the 11.35am from Redhill formed of seven
coaches — instead of the usual three or four —
on 1 January 1965. *Brian Stephenson*

BELOW: 'County' class 4-6-0 No 1025 *County Radnor* arrives at Chester General with a stopping train from Shrewsbury in the early 1950s. *Kenneth Field*

5 The 'Counties'

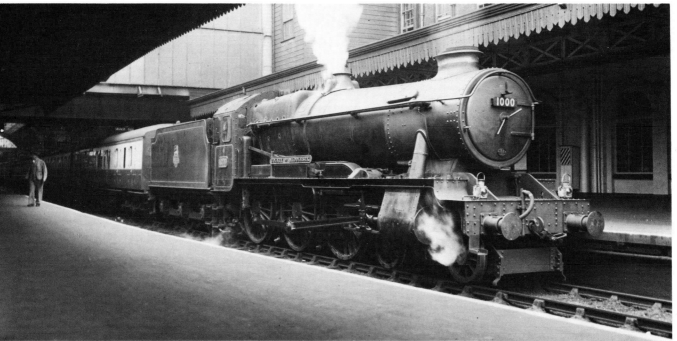

UPPER LEFT: 'County' No 1004 *County of Somerset* descends the bank at Tomperro between
...acewater and Truro with an up freight on 8 May 1947. *B. A. Butt*

...WER LEFT: A relief portion of the 2.10pm Paddington-Birkenhead express passes Gerrards Cross
...ind No 1029 *County of Worcester* in 1947. *C. R. L. Coles*

...P: No 1017 *County of Hereford* heads away from Chester with an express for Paddington on
...August 1946. *Eric Treacy*

...OVE: The prototype 'County' No 1000 *County of Middlesex*, still fitted with its original large double
...mney, waits to leave Paddington with a West of England train on 8 July 1952. *John P. Wilson*

UPPER LEFT: The 'County' 4-6-0s were always a familiar sight on Cornwall's main line. Here, appropriately, No 1006 *County of Cornwall* arrives at Lostwithiel with the 11.05am Plymouth-Penzance stopping train on 14 June 1956. *M. Mensing*

LOWER LEFT: The up 'Cornish Riveria Express' pauses at Truro with No 1015 *County of Gloucester*, Laira shed in charge. *Lens of Sutton*

ABOVE: No 1010 *County of Caernarvon* toils up the 1 in 70 of Doublebois bank near Largin signalbox with the 11.50am Penzance-Paddington express on 25 August 1956. *Peter F. Bowles*

LEFT: Here fitted with a double chimney, No 1007 *County of Brecknock* climbs away fro[m] Truro with the 4.15pm stopping train to Penzan[ce] on 16 May 1959. Double chimneys were fitted [to] all 30 County 4-6-0s between May 1956 and October 1959. *M. Mensing*

BELOW: The 10.15am Penzance-Manchester train arrives at Plymouth North Road behind No 1006 *County of Cornwall* on 16 May 1954. *R. E. Vincent*

UPPER RIGHT: Almost at the end of steam i[n] the West Country No 1009 *County of Carmarthen* pilots 'Warship' class diesel-hydraulic B-B No D823 *Hermes* down Rattery bank between Brent and Totnes with the 10.05a[m] Penzance-Liverpool train on 28 July 1962. *D. Ian Wood*

LOWER RIGHT: No 1019 *County of Merione[th]* pilots a Collett 2-6-2T on the Saturday 10.05am Penzance-Liverpool train seen passing Aller Junction, Newton Abbot, in July 1957. *Derek Cross*

107

UPPER LEFT: No 1009 *County of Carmarthen* climbs the 1 in 73 gradient out of Torre with the Saturday 8.52am Paignton-Sheffield train on 13 July 1957. *Peter F. Bowles*

LOWER LEFT: Shrewsbury's No 1017 *County of Hereford* waits to leave Bristol Temple Meads with the Saturday 2.55pm Paignton-Wolverhampton train on 7 July 1956. *John P. Wilson*

RIGHT: The 7.30am Paddington-Plymouth express leaves Parsons Tunnel hauled by No 1009 *County of Carmarthen* on 16 April 1957. *W. N. Lockett*

BELOW: No 1011 *County of Chester* leaves Dawlish with the Saturday 10.58am Paignton-Nottingham train in September 1959. *Derek Cross*

ABOVE: A stopping train from Shrewsbury approaches Chester hauled by
No 1013 *County of Dorset* **about 1960.** *Kenneth Field*

UPPER RIGHT: No 1005 *County of Devon* **tops the bank from Stratford-
upon-Avon at Wilmcote with a Bristol-Birmingham football special on
16 February 1957.** *T. E. Williams*

RIGHT: A slow train from Chester enters Shrewsbury behind No 1003
County of Wilts **on 13 June 1957. It was a strange fact that few of the
'Counties' were allocated to depots in the county after which they were
named. Certainly one would have thought** *County of Wilts* **would have been
a Swindon loco.** *R. O. Tuck*

PPER LEFT: No 1016 *County of Hants* coasts ⟨dow⟩n Nantyderry bank to Penpergwm with the ⟨9.0⟩am Plymouth-Manchester train on 10 August ⟨195⟩7. This engine was working through from ⟨New⟩ton Abbot to Shrewsbury on a double home ⟨log⟩ging turn from the latter depot. *R. O. Tuck*

⟨LO⟩WER LEFT: No 1020 *County of Monmouth* ⟨clim⟩bs away from Haverfordwest with the ⟨8.4⟩0pm Neyland-Paddington train on 5 August ⟨195⟩1. *J. F. Aylard*

⟨RI⟩GHT: The 1.55pm Paddington-Swansea ⟨exp⟩ress passes under the Barry Railway Viaduct ⟨eas⟩t of St Fagans unusually hauled by County ⟨4-6-⟩0 No 1011 *County of Chester* on 6 June ⟨195⟩9. *R. O. Tuck*

⟨BE⟩LOW: No 1029 *County of Worcester* and a ⟨sist⟩er engine rest at their home shed of Neyland in ⟨the ⟩middle 1950s. *Lens of Sutton*

TOP: No 1015 *County of Gloucester* **heads a Weymouth-Bristol train west of Bathampton in June 1960.** *Derek Cross*

ABOVE: A Bristol-Weymouth train leaves Bincombe Tunnel behind No 1027 *County of Stafford* **on a wet day in July 1960.** *Derek Cross*

UPPER RIGHT: A nicely turned-out No 1011 *County of Chester* **takes water from Keynsham troughs with the 12.50pm Cardiff-Brighton train on 30 April 1960.** *W. N. Lockett*

LOWER RIGHT: Storm clouds are brewing as No 1009 *County of Carmarthen* **climbs away from Weymouth in September 1957 with the 4.05pm Weymouth Quay-Cardiff and Birmingham train.** *T. G. Hepburn/Rail Archive Stephenson*

TOP: No 1021 *County of Montgomery* leaves Hereford with the Sunday 10.30am Liverpool-Plymouth express on 25 June 1961. *Ivo Peters*

ABOVE: Newly fitted with a double chimney, No 1016 *County of Hants* stands in the centre road at Bath Spa station while on a running-in turn from Swindon in 1957. *Ivo Peters*

UPPER RIGHT: A Sunday evening Taunton-Paddington train leaves Bath behind No 1006 *County of Cornwall* on 13 August 1961. *Derek Cross*

RIGHT: No 1029 *County of Worcester* climbs towards Bruton with an up unfitted freight on 22 September 1961. Although designated mixed traffic engines the 'Counties' were seldom seen on freight workings except those of an express nature such as milk or fish trains. *Patrick Russell*

BELOW: No 1028 *County of Warwick* climbs Hatton bank with a down fitted freight on 28 September 1963. *Paul Riley*

UPPER RIGHT: The 3.50pm Whitland-Kensington milk train is diverted through the up goods loop at Pengam Junction, Cardiff, hauled by No 1019 *County of Merioneth* on 19 July 1962. *R. O. Tuck*

LOWER RIGHT: The last 'County' in service, No 1011 *County of Chester* is swathed in steam as it climbs Sapperton bank with an SLS special from Birmingham to Swindon on 20 September 1964. It was withdrawn in November 1964. Alas, none of the 'Counties' ended up in Barry scrapyard to slumber for years and then arise phoenix-like, leaving a large gap in the ranks of preserved GWR locomotives. *Gerald T. Robinson*

119

LEFT: After languishing at Swindon for many years after withdrawal 'Star' No 4003 *Lode Star* was restored to its former glory for inclusion in the Great Western Railway Museum at Swindon. Here it is on a Pickfords low loader in Swindon goods yard before being moved into the museum on 29 April 1962. *M. Pope*

GREAT WESTERN RAILWAY 4-6-0 s
Summary of numbers and dates
'Saint' Class

Pre-1913 No	No	Name	*Swindon Works No	Date Built	Rebuilt From 4-4-2	Date Withdrawn	Notes
100	2900	*William Dean*	1928	2/02	—	6/32	1
	2901	*Lady Superior*	2199	5/06	—	4/33	
	2902	*Lady of the Lake*	2200	5/06	—	8/49	
	2903	*Lady of Lyons*	2201	5/06	—	11/49	
	2904	*Lady Godiva*	2202	5/06	—	10/32	
	2905	*Lady Macbeth*	2203	5/06	—	4/48	
	2906	*Lady of Lynn*	2204	5/06	—	8/52	
	2907	*Lady Disdain*	2205	5/06	—	7/33	
	2908	*Lady of Quality*	2206	5/06	—	12/50	
	2909	*Lady of Provence*	2207	5/06	—	11/31	
	2910	*Lady of Shalott*	2208	5/06	—	10/31	
	2911	*Saint Agatha*	2259	8/07	—	3/35	
	2912	*Saint Ambrose*	2260	8/07	—	2/51	
	2913	*Saint Andrew*	2261	8/07	—	5/48	
	2914	*Saint Augustine*	2262	8/07	—	1/46	
	2915	*Saint Bartholomew*	2263	8/07	—	10/50	
	2916	*Saint Benedict*	2264	8/07	—	7/48	
	2917	*Saint Bernard*	2265	8/07	—	10/34	
	2918	*Saint Catherine*	2266	8/07	—	2/35	
	2919	*Saint Cuthbert*	2267	9/07	—	2/32	2
	2920	*Saint David*	2268	9/07	—	10/53	
	2921	*Saint Dunstan*	2269	9/07	—	12/45	
	2922	*Saint Gabriel*	2270	9/07	—	12/44	
	2923	*Saint George*	2271	9/07	—	10/34	
	2924	*Saint Helena*	2272	9/07	—	3/50	
	2925	*Saint Martin*	2273	9/07	—	12/24	3
	2926	*Saint Nicholas*	2274	9/07	—	9/51	
	2927	*Saint Patrick*	2275	9/07	—	12/51	
	2928	*Saint Sebastian*	2276	9/07	—	8/48	
	2929	*Saint Stephen*	2277	9/07	—	12/49	
	2930	*Saint Vincent*	2278	9/07	—	10/49	
	2931	*Arlington Court*	(2426)	10/11	—	2/51	
	2932	*Ashton Court*	(2427)	10/11	—	6/51	
	2933	*Bibury Court*	(2428)	11/11	—	1/53	
	2934	*Butleigh Court*	(2429)	11/11	—	6/52	
	2935	*Caynham Court*	(2430)	11/11	—	12/48	4
	2936	*Cefntilla Court*	(2431)	11/11	—	4/51	
	2937	*Clevedon Court*	(2432)	12/11	—	6/53	
	2938	*Corsham Court*	(2433)	12/11	—	8/52	
	2939	*Croome Court*	(2434)	12/11	—	12/50	
	2940	*Dorney Court*	(2435)	12/11	—	1/52	
	2941	*Easton Court*	(2476)	5/12	—	12/49	
	2942	*Fawley Court*	(2477)	5/12	—	12/49	
	2943	*Hampton Court*	(2478)	5/12	—	1/51	
	2944	*Highnam Court*	(2479)	5/12	—	11/51	
	2945	*Hillingdon Court*	(2480)	6/12	—	6/53	
	2946	*Langford Court*	(2481)	6/12	—	11/49	
	2947	*Madresfield Court*	(2482)	6/12	—	4/51	
	2948	*Stackpole Court*	(2483)	6/12	—	11/51	
	2949	*Stanford Court*	(2484)	5/12	—	1/52	
	2950	*Taplow Court*	(2485)	5/12	—	9/52	
	2951	*Tawstock Court*	(2506)	3/13	—	6/52	
	2952	*Twineham Court*	(2507)	3/13	—	9/51	
	2953	*Titley Court*	(2508)	3/13	—	2/52	
	2954	*Tockenham Court*	(2509)	3/13	—	7/52	
	2955	*Tortworth Court*	(2510)	4/13	—	3/50	
171	2971	*Albion*	2024	12/03	7/07	1/46	5
172	2972	*The Abbot*	2106	2/05	4/12	3/35	6
173	2973	*Robins Bolitho*	2107	3/05	—	7/33	

Pre-1913 No	No	Name	*Swindon Works No	Date Built	Date Rebuilt From 4-4-2	Date Withdrawn	Notes
174	2974	*Lord Barrymore*	2108	3/05	—	8/33	7
175	2975	*Lord Palmer*	2109	3/05	—	11/44	8
176	2976	*Winterstoke*	2110	4/05	—	1/34	
177	2977	*Robertson*	2111	4/05	—	2/35	
178	2978	*Kirkland*	2112	4/05	—	8/46	9
179	2979	*Quentin Durward*	2113	4/05	8/12	1/51	10
180	2980	*Coeur de Lion*	2114	5/05	1/13	5/48	
181	2981	*Ivanhoe*	2128	6/05	7/12	3/51	
182	2982	*Lalla Rookh*	2129	6/05	11/12	6/34	
183	2983	*Redgauntlet*	2130	7/05	4/12	3/46	
184	2984	*Guy Mannering*	2131	7/05	8/12	5/33	11
185	2985	*Peveril of the Peak*	2132	7/05	8/12	8/31	12
186	2986	*Robin Hood*	2133	7/05	5/12	11/32	
187	2987	*Bride of Lammermoor*	2134	8/05	6/12	10/49	13
188	2988	*Rob Roy*	2135	8/05	5/12	5/48	
189	2989	*Talisman*	2136	9/05	10/12	9/48	
190	2990	*Waverley*	2137	9/05	11/12	1/39	
98	2998	*Ernest Cunard*	1990	3/03	—	6/33	14

'Star' Class

No	Name	*Swindon Works No	Date Built	Date Withdrawn	Notes	No	Name	*Swindon Works No	Date Built	Date Withdrawn	Notes
4000	*North Star*	2168	4/06	11/29	15, 16	4036	*Queen Elizabeth*	2385	12/10	3/52	
4001	*Dog Star*	2229	2/07	1/34		4037	*Queen Philippa*	2386	12/10	6/26	16
4002	*Evening Star*	2230	3/07	6/33		4038	*Queen Berengaria*	2387	1/11	4/52	
4003	*Lode Star*	2231	2/07	7/51	17	4039	*Queen Matilda*	2388	2/11	11/50	
4004	*Morning Star*	2232	2/07	4/48		4040	*Queen Boadicea*	2389	3/11	6/51	
4005	*Polar Star*	2233	2/07	11/34		4041	*Prince of Wales*	(2536)	6/13	4/51	
4006	*Red Star*	2234	4/07	11/32		4042	*Prince Albert*	(2537)	5/13	11/51	
4007	*Rising Star*	2235	4/07	9/51	18	4043	*Prince Henry*	(2538)	5/13	1/52	
4008	*Royal Star*	2236	5/07	6/35		4044	*Prince George*	(2539)	5/13	2/53	
4009	*Shooting Star*	2237	5/07	4/25	16	4045	*Prince John*	(2540)	6/13	11/50	
4010	*Western Star*	2238	5/07	11/34		4046	*Princess Mary*	(2572)	5/14	11/51	
4011	*Knight of the Garter*	2300	3/08	11/32		4047	*Princess Louise*	(2573)	5/14	7/51	
4012	*Knight of the Thistle*	2301	3/08	10/49		4048	*Princess Victoria*	(2574)	5/14	1/53	
4013	*Knight of St Patrick*	2302	3/08	5/50		4049	*Princess Maud*	(2575)	5/14	7/53	
4014	*Knight of the Bath*	2303	3/08	6/46		4050	*Princess Alice*	(2576)	6/14	2/52	
4015	*Knight of St John*	2304	3/08	2/51		4051	*Princess Helena*	(2577)	6/14	10/50	
4016	*Knight of the Golden Fleece*	2305	4/08	10/25	16	4052	*Princess Beatrice*	(2578)	6/14	6/53	
4017	*Knight of the Black Eagle*	2306	4/08	11/49	19	4053	*Princess Alexandra*	(2579)	6/14	7/54	
4018	*Knight of the Grand Cross*	2307	4/08	4/51		4054	*Princess Charlotte*	(2580)	6/14	2/52	
4019	*Knight Templar*	2308	5/08	10/49		4055	*Princess Sophia*	(2581)	7/14	2/51	
4020	*Knight Commander*	2309	5/08	3/51		4056	*Princess Margaret*	(2582)	7/14	10/57	
4021	*King Edward*	2365	6/09	10/52	20	4057	*Princess Elizabeth*	(2583)	7/14	2/52	
4022	*King William*	2366	6/09	2/52	20	4058	*Princess Augusta*	(2584)	7/14	4/51	
4023	*King George*	2367	6/09	7/52	20	4059	*Princess Patricia*	(2585)	7/14	9/52	
4024	*King James*	2368	6/09	2/35	20	4060	*Princess Eugenie*	(2586)	7/14	9/52	
4025	*King Charles*	2369	7/09	8/50	20	4061	*Glastonbury Abbey*	(2915)	5/22	3/57	
4026	*King Richard*	2370	9/09	2/50	20	4062	*Malmesbury Abbey*	(2916)	5/22	11/56	
4027	*King Henry*	2371	9/09	10/34	20	4063	*Bath Abbey*	(2917)	11/22	3/37	16
4028	*King John*	2372	9/09	11/51	20	4064	*Reading Abbey*	(2918)	12/22	2/37	16
4029	*King Stephen*	2373	10/09	11/34	20	4065	*Evesham Abbey*	(2919)	12/22	3/39	16
4030	*King Harold*	2374	10/09	5/50	20	4066	*Malvern Abbey*	(2920)	12/22	12/37	16, 21
4031	*Queen Mary*	2380	10/10	6/51		4067	*Tintern Abbey*	(2921)	1/23	9/40	16
4032	*Queen Alexandra*	2381	10/10	4/26	16	4068	*Llanthony Abbey*	(2922)	1/23	11/38	16
4033	*Queen Victoria*	2382	11/10	6/51		4069	*Westminster Abbey*	(2923)	1/23	4/39	16, 22
4034	*Queen Adelaide*	2383	11/10	9/52		4070	*Neath Abbey*	(2924)	2/23	1/39	16
4035	*Queen Charlotte*	2384	11/10	10/51		4071	*Cleeve Abbey*	(2925)	2/23	9/38	16
						4072	*Tresco Abbey*	(2926)	2/23	3/38	16

*The Works Numbers in brackets were not carried by the locomotive.

Notes:

1. The first Churchward 4-6-0, named *Dean* in 6/02 and altered to *William Dean* in 11/02.
2. Was named *Saint Cecilia* until 10/07.
3. Rebuilt as the prototype 'Hall' class 4-6-0.
4. Fitted with rotary cam poppet valve gear in 5/31.
5. Was rebuilt as a 4-4-2 in 10/04 reverting to a 4-6-0 as shown. It was renamed *The Pirate* from 3/07 to 7/07.
6. Was named *Quicksilver* until 3/07.
7. Was named *Barrymore* until 5/05.
8. Was first named *Viscount Churchill* in 1907, renamed *Sir Ernest Palmer* from 2/24 until 10/33.
9. Was renamed *Charles J. Hambro* in 5/35.
10. Was named *Magnet* until 3/07.
11. Was first named *Churchill*, altered to *Viscount Churchill* in 1906, and renamed *Guy Mannering* in 1907.
12. Was named *Winterstoke* until 4/07.
13. Was named *Robertson* until 4/07.
14. Was first named *Vanguard* in 3/07 and renamed *Ernest Cunard* in 12/07.
15. Built as a 4-4-2, rebuilt as a 4-6-0 in 11/06.
16. Rebuilt as a 'Castle' Class 4-6-0.

Notes:

17. Preserved in Great Western Railway Museum, Swindon.
18. Renamed *Swallowfield Park* in 5/37.
19. Renamed *Knight of Liege* in 8/14.
20. When the 'King' class was introduced in 1927, Nos 4021-30 were renamed as follows:
    4021 *The British Monarch* 6/27
    4022 *The Belgian Monarch* 6/27
    4023 *The Danish Monarch* 7/27
    4024 *The Dutch Monarch* 9/27
    4025 *Italian Monarch* 10/27
    4026 *The Japanese Monarch* 7/27
    4027 *The Norwegian Monarch* 7/27
    4028 *The Roumanian Monarch* 7/27
    4029 *The Spanish Monarch* 7/27
    4030 *The Swedish Monarch* 7/27
    Nos 4021-24/26-30 were fitted with altered nameplates ommitting the word 'The' in Oct/Nov 1927. The names of Nos 4022/23/25/26/28/30 were removed in 1940/41.
21. Renamed *Sir Robert Horne* in 5/35, altered to *Viscount Horne* in 8/37.
22. Named *Margam Abbey* until 5/23.

'CASTLE' CLASS

GWR No	Final name	Previous name and date of change	Date built/ rebuilt	Double chimney fitted	Date with- drawn	Shed Allocation 5/53	Final Shed	Notes
100 A1	Lloyd's	Shooting Star 1/36	4/25	—	3/50	—	Old Oak Common	1, 2
111	Viscount Churchill		9/24	—	7/53	Laira	Old Oak Common	3
4000	North Star		11/29	—	5/57	Wolverhampton	Landore	1
4016	The Somerset Light Infantry (Prince Albert's)	Knight of the Golden Fleece 1/38	10/25	—	9/51	—	Old Oak Common	1
4032	Queen Alexandra		4/26	—	9/51	—	Taunton	1
4037	The South Wales Borderers	Queen Philippa 3/37	6/26	—	9/62	Old Oak Common	Exeter	1
4073	Caerphilly Castle		8/23	—	5/60	St Philip's Marsh	Cardiff Canton	4
4074	Caldicot Castle		12/23	4/59	5/63	Landore	Old Oak Common	
4075	Cardiff Castle		1/24	—	11/61	St Philip's Marsh	Old Oak Common	
4076	Carmarthen Castle		2/24	—	2/63	Chester	Llanelly	
4077	Chepstow Castle		2/24	—	8/62	Newton Abbot	St Philip's Marsh	
4078	Pembroke Castle		2/24	—	7/62	Landore	Llanelly	
4079	Pendennis Castle		2/24	—	5/64	Wolverhampton	St Philip's Marsh	5
4080	Powderham Castle		3/24	8/58	8/64	Westbury	Southall	
4081	Warwick Castle		3/24	—	1/63	Landore	Carmarthen	
4082	Windsor Castle		4/24	—	9/64	Old Oak Common	Gloucester	6
4083	Abbotsbury Castle		5/25	—	12/61	Wolverhampton	Cardiff Canton	
4084	Aberystwyth Castle		5/25	—	10/60	Bristol Bath Rd	Cardiff Canton	
4085	Berkeley Castle		5/25	—	5/62	Reading	Old Oak Common	
4086	Builth Castle		6/25	—	4/62	Laira	Reading	
4087	Cardigan Castle		6/25	2/58	10/63	Penzance	St Philip's Marsh	
4088	Dartmouth Castle		7/25	5/58	5/64	Laira	St Philip's Marsh	
4089	Donnington Castle		7/25	—	9/64	Laira	Southall	
4090	Dorchester Castle		7/25	4/57	6/63	Old Oak Common	Cardiff East Dock	
4091	Dudley Castle		7/25	—	1/59	Bristol Bath Rd	Old Oak Common	
4092	Dunraven Castle		8/25	—	12/61	Wolverhampton	Oxford	
4093	Dunster Castle		5/26	12/57	9/64	Landore	Gloucester	
4094	Dynevor Castle		5/26	—	3/62	Bristol Bath Rd	Carmarthen	
4095	Harlech Castle		6/26	—	12/62	Landore	Reading	
4096	Highclere Castle		6/26	—	1/63	Bristol Bath Rd	Old Oak Common	
4097	Kenilworth Castle		6/26	6/58	5/60	Old Oak Common	Landore	
4098	Kidwelly Castle		7/26	—	12/63	Newton Abbot	Old Oak Common	
4099	Kilgerran Castle		8/26	—	9/62	Newton Abbot	Llanelly	
5000	Launceston Castle		9/26	—	10/64	Bristol Bath Rd	Oxley	
5001	Llandovery Castle		9/26	7/61	2/63	Cardiff Canton	Old Oak Common	
5002	Ludlow Castle		9/26	—	9/64	Landore	Southall	
5003	Lulworth Castle		5/27	—	8/62	Exeter	Newton Abbot	
5004	Llanstephan Castle		6/27	—	4/62	Old Oak Common	Neath	
5005	Manorbier Castle		6/27	—	2/60	Cardiff Canton	Swindon	7
5006	Tregenna Castle		6/27	—	4/62	Cardiff Canton	Carmarthen	
5007	Rougemont Castle		6/27	—	9/62	Cardiff Canton	Gloucester	
5008	Raglan Castle		6/27	3/61	9/62	Wolverhampton	Old Oak Common	
5009	Shrewsbury Castle		6/27	—	10/60	Swindon	Swindon	
5010	Restormel Castle		7/27	—	10/59	Wolverhampton	Reading	
5011	Tintagel Castle		7/27	—	9/62	Newton Abbot	Old Oak Common	
5012	Berry Pomeroy Castle		7/27	—	4/62	Oxford	Oxford	
5013	Abergavenny Castle		6/32	—	7/62	Old Oak Common	Neath	
5014	Goodrich Castle		6/32	—	2/65	Old Oak Common	Tyseley	
5015	Kingswear Castle		7/32	—	4/63	Bristol Bath Rd	Cardiff East Dock	
5016	Montgomery Castle		7/32	2/61	9/62	Landore	Llanelly	
5017	The Gloucestershire Regiment 28th 61st	St.Donats Castle 4/54	7/32	—	9/62	Gloucester	Gloucester	
5018	St.Mawes Castle		7/32	—	3/64	Gloucester	Reading	
5019	Treago Castle		7/32	3/61	9/62	Bristol Bath Rd	Wolverhampton	
5020	Trematon Castle		7/32	—	11/62	Cardiff Canton	Llanelly	
5021	Whittington Castle		8/32	—	9/62	Exeter	Cardiff Canton	
5022	Wigmore Castle		8/32	2/59	6/63	Wolverhampton	Wolverhampton	
5023	Brecon Castle		4/34	—	2/63	Penzance	Swindon	
5024	Carew Castle		4/34	—	5/62	Newton Abbot	Newton Abbot	
5025	Chirk Castle		4/34	—	11/63	Bristol Bath Rd	Hereford	
5026	Criccieth Castle		4/34	10/59	11/64	Oxford	Tyseley	
5027	Farleigh Castle		4/34	4/61	11/62	Wolverhampton	Llanelly	
5028	Llantilio Castle		5/34	—	5/60	Newton Abbot	Laira	
5029	Nunney Castle		5/34	—	12/63	Old Oak Common	Cardiff East Dock	8
5030	Shirburn Castle		5/34	—	9/62	Cardiff Canton	Carmarthen	
5031	Totnes Castle		5/34	6/59	10/63	Wolverhampton	Oxley	
5032	Usk Castle		5/34	5/59	9/62	Wolverhampton	Old Oak Common	
5033	Broughton Castle		5/35	10/60	9/62	Chester	Oxford	
5034	Corfe Castle		5/35	2/61	9/62	Reading	Old Oak Common	
5035	Coity Castle		5/35	—	5/62	Old Oak Common	Swindon	
5036	Lyonshall Castle		5/35	12/60	9/62	Reading	Old Oak Common	
5037	Monmouth Castle		5/35	—	3/64	Bristol Bath Rd	St Philip's Marsh	
5038	Morlais Castle		6/35	—	9/63	Old Oak Common	Reading	
5039	Rhuddlan Castle		6/35	—	6/64	Carmarthen	Reading	
5040	Stokesay Castle		6/35	—	10/63	Old Oak Common	St Philip's Marsh	
5041	Tiverton Castle		7/35	—	12/63	Newton Abbot	Old Oak Common	
5042	Winchester Castle		7/35	—	6/65	Gloucester	Gloucester	
5043	Earl of Mount Edgcumbe	Barbury Castle 9/37	3/36	5/58	12/63	Carmarthen	Cardiff East Dock	13
5044	Earl of Dunraven	Beverston Castle 9/37	3/36	—	4/62	Old Oak Common	Cardiff Canton	
5045	Earl of Dudley	Bridgwater Castle 9/37	3/36	—	9/62	Bristol Bath Rd	Wolverhampton	
5046	Earl Cawdor	Clifford Castle 8/37	4/36	—	9/62	Cardiff Canton	Wolverhampton	
5047	Earl of Dartmouth	Compton Castle 8/37	4/36	—	9/62	Newton Abbot	Wolverhampton	
5048	Earl of Devon	Cranbrook Castle 8/37	4/36	—	8/62	Bristol Bath Rd	Llanelly	
5049	Earl of Plymouth	Denbigh Castle 8/37	4/36	9/59	3/63	Cardiff Canton	St Philip's Marsh	
5050	Earl of St. Germans	Devizes Castle 8/37	5/36	—	8/63	Shrewsbury	St Philip's Marsh	
5051	Earl Bathurst	Drysllwyn Castle 8/37	5/36	—	5/63	Landore	Llanelly	9
5052	Earl of Radnor	Eastnor Castle 7/37	5/36	—	9/62	Cardiff Canton	St Philip's Marsh	
5053	Earl Cairns	Bishop's Castle 8/37	5/36	—	7/62	Bristol bath Rd	Cardiff Canton	
5054	Earl of Ducie	Lamphey Castle 9/37	6/36	—	10/64	Cardiff Canton	Gloucester	
5055	Earl of Eldon	Lydford Castle 8/37	6/36	—	9/64	Old Oak Common	Gloucester	
5056	Earl of Powis	Ogmore Castle 9/37	6/36	11/60	11/64	Old Oak Common	Tyseley	
5057	Earl Waldegrave	Penrice Castle 10/37	6/36	5/58	3/64	Laira	Old Oak Common	
5058	Earl of Clancarty	Newport Castle 9/37	5/37	—	3/63	Laira	Gloucester	
5059	Earl St. Aldwyn	Powis Castle 10/37	5/37	—	6/62	Exeter	Shrewsbury	
5060	Earl of Berkeley	Sarum Castle 10/37	6/37	8/61	4/63	Old Oak Common	Old Oak Common	
5061	Earl of Birkenhead	Sudeley Castle 10/37	6/37	9/58	9/62	Chester	Cardiff Canton	

122

GWR No	Final name	Previous name and date of change	Date built/ rebuilt	Double chimney fitted	Date withdrawn	Shed Allocation 5/53	Final Shed	Notes
5062	Earl of Shaftesbury	Tenby Castle 11/37	6/37	—	8/62	Swindon	Llanelly	
5063	Earl Baldwin	Thornbury Castle 7/37	6/37	—	2/65	Worcester	Oxley	
5064	Bishop's Castle	Tretower Castle 9/37	6/37	9/58	9/62	Bristol Bath Rd	Gloucester	
5065	Newport Castle	Upton Castle 9/37	7/37	—	1/63	Old Oak Common	Old Oak Common	
5066	Sir Felix Pole	Wardour Castle 4/56	7/37	4/59	9/62	Old Oak Common	Old Oak Common	
5067	St. Fagans Castle		7/37	—	7/62	Bristol Bath Rd	Reading	
5068	Beverston Castle		6/38	3/61	9/62	Swindon	Oxford	
5069	Isambard Kingdom Brunel		6/38	11/58	2/62	Bristol Bath Rd	Laira	
5070	Sir Daniel Gooch		6/38	—	3/64	Wolverhampton	Old Oak Common	
5071	Spitfire	Clifford Castle 9/40	6/38	6/59	10/63	Newton Abbot	St Philip's Marsh	
5072	Hurricane	Compton Castle 11/40	6/38	—	10/62	Landore	Wolverhampton	
5073	Blenheim	Cranbrook Castle 1/41	7/38	7/59	2/64	Shrewsbury	Cardiff East Dock	
5074	Hampden	Denbigh Castle 1/41	7/38	9/61	5/64	Bristol Bath Rd	St Philip's Marsh	
5075	Wellington	Devizes Castle 10/40	8/38	—	9/62	Chester	St Philip's Marsh	
5076	Gladiator	Drysllwyn Castle 1/41	8/38	—	9/64	Bristol Bath Rd	Southall	
5077	Fairey Battle	Eastnor Castle 10/40	8/38	—	7/62	Cardiff Canton	Llanelly	
5078	Beaufort	Lamphey Castle 1/41	5/39	12/61	11/62	Newton Abbot	Neath	
5079	Lysander	Lydford Castle 11/40	5/39	—	5/60	Newton Abbot	Newton Abbot	
5080	Defiant	Ogmore Castle 1/41	5/39	—	4/63	Cardiff Canton	Llanelly	13
5081	Lockheed Hudson	Penrice Castle 1/41	5/39	—	10/63	Old Oak Common	Cardiff East Dock	
5082	Swordfish	Powis Castle 1/41	6/39	—	7/62	Old Oak Common	Old Oak Common	
5083	Bath Abbey		6/37	—	1/59	Swindon	Worcester	1
5084	Reading Abbey		4/37	10/58	7/62	Swindon	Old Oak Common	1
5085	Evesham Abbey		7/39	—	2/64	Bristol Bath Rd	St Philip's Marsh	1
5086	Viscount Horne		12/37	—	11/58	Worcester	Worcester	1
5087	Tintern Abbey		11/40	—	8/63	Old Oak Common	Llanelly	1
5088	Llanthony Abbey		2/39	6/58	9/62	Wolverhampton	Wolverhampton	1
5089	Westminster Abbey		10/39	—	11/64	Cardiff Canton	Tyseley	1
5090	Neath Abbey		4/39	—	5/62	Worcester	Old Oak Common	1
5091	Cleeve Abbey		12/38	—	10/64	Swindon	Tyseley	1
5092	Tresco Abbey		4/38	10/61	7/63	Worcester	Cardiff East Dock	1
5093	Upton Castle		6/39	—	9/63	Old Oak Common	Old Oak Common	
5094	Tretower Castle		6/39	6/60	9/62	Bristol Bath Rd	St Philip's Marsh	
5095	Barbury Castle		6/39	11/58	8/62	Old Oak Common	Shrewsbury	
5096	Bridgwater Castle		6/39	—	6/64	Bristol Bath Rd	Worcester	
5097	Sarum Castle		7/39	7/61	3/63	Shrewsbury	Cardiff East Dock	
5098	Clifford Castle		5/46	1/59	6/64	Laira	Reading	
5099	Compton Castle		5/46	—	2/63	Cardiff Canton	Gloucester	
7000	Viscount Portal		5/46	—	12/63	Newton Abbot	Worcester	
7001	Sir James Milne	Denbigh Castle 2/48	5/46	9/60	9/63	Old Oak Common	Oxley	
7002	Devizes Castle		6/46	7/61	3/64	Landore	Worcester	
7003	Elmley Castle		6/46	6/60	8/64	Landore	Gloucester	
7004	Eastnor Castle		6/46	2/58	1/64	Old Oak Common	Reading	
7005	Sir Edward Elgar	Lamphey Castle 8/57	6/46	—	9/64	Worcester	Southall	
7006	Lydford Castle		6/46	6/60	12/63	Gloucester	Old Oak Common	
7007	Great Western	Ogmore Castle 1/48	7/46	6/61	2/63	Worcester	Worcester	
7008	Swansea Castle		5/48	6/59	9/64	Oxford	Old Oak Common	
7009	Athelney Castle		5/48	—	3/63	Llanelly	Old Oak Common	
7010	Avondale Castle		6/48	10/60	3/64	Old Oak Common	Reading	
7011	Banbury Castle		6/48	—	2/65	Bristol Bath Rd	Oxley	
7012	Barry Castle		6/48	—	11/64	Landore	Tyseley	
7013	Bristol Castle		7/48	5/58	2/65	Worcester	Tyseley	10
7014	Caerhays Castle		7/48	2/59	2/65	Bristol Bath Road	Tyseley	
7015	Carn Brea Castle		7/48	5/59	4/63	Swindon	Old Oak Common	
7016	Chester Castle		8/48	—	11/62	Cardiff Canton	Cardiff East Dock	
7017	G. J. Churchward		8/48	—	2/63	Cardiff Canton	Old Oak Common	
7018	Drysllwyn Castle		5/49	4/58	9/63	Landore	Old Oak Common	
7019	Fowey Castle		5/49	9/58	2/65	Bristol Bath Road	Oxley	
7020	Gloucester Castle		5/49	2/61	9/64	Cardiff Canton	Southall	
7021	Haverfordwest Castle		6/49	11/61	9/63	Llanelly	Old Oak Common	
7022	Hereford Castle		6/49	1/58	6/65	Cardiff Canton	Gloucester	
7023	Penrice Castle		6/49	5/58	2/65	Cardiff Canton	Oxley	
7024	Powis Castle		6/49	3/59	2/65	Old Oak Common	Oxley	
7025	Sudeley Castle		8/49	—	9/64	Old Oak Common	Worcester	
7026	Tenby Castle		8/49	—	10/64	Wolverhampton	Tyseley	
7027	Thornbury Castle		8/49	—	12/63	Old Oak Common	Reading	11
7028	Cadbury Castle		5/50	10/61	12/63	Landore	Llanelly	
7029	Clun Castle		5/50	10/59	12/65	Newton Abbot	Gloucester	12
7030	Cranbrook Castle		6/50	7/59	2/63	Old Oak Common	Old Oak Common	
7031	Cromwell's Castle		6/50	—	7/63	Laira	Worcester	
7032	Denbigh Castle		6/50	9/60	9/64	Old Oak Common	Old Oak Common	
7033	Hartlebury Castle		7/50	7/59	1/63	Old Oak Common	Old Oak Common	
7034	Ince Castle		8/50	12/59	6/65	Bristol Bath Rd	Gloucester	
7035	Ogmore Castle		8/50	1/60	6/64	Shrewsbury	Old Oak Common	
7036	Taunton Castle		8/50	8/59	9/63	Old Oak Common	Old Oak Common	
7037	Swindon		8/50	—	3/63	Swindon	Old Oak Common	

NOTES: All locomotives built or rebuilt at Swindon

) Rebuilt from Churchward 'Star' class 4-6-0.

) Originally No 4009 *Shooting Star* and was renamed and numbered 100 A1 *Lloyds* in 1936.

) Nominally a rebuild of the Churchward Pacific No 111 *The Great Bear*.

) Prototype 'Castle' now preserved at the Science Museum, London.

) Privately preserved by Hammersley Iron at Dampier, Australia.

) This engine exchanged identities with No 7013 in February 1952, the withdrawal date is that of the original No 7013.

) Semi-streamlined in February 1935, parts of this were removed in September 1935, the bullnose in 1943 and the final trace, the wedge-shaped cab, was removed in 1947.

) Purchased in 1973 from Woodham Bros at Barry for Great Western Society, Didcot.

) Restored by the Great Western Society at Didcot after rescue from Barry scrapyard in 1969.

) This engine exchanged identities with No 4082 in February 1952, the withdrawal date is that of the original No 4082.

) Being restored by the Standard Gauge Steam Trust at Tyseley after rescue from Barry scrapyard in 1972.

) Preserved in working order by the Standard Gauge Steam Trust at Tyseley.

) Purchased from Woodham Bros for use as spare parts by the Standard Gauge Steam Trust at Tyseley.

LEFT: The preserved 'King' No 6000 *King George V* climbs Coton Hill bank out of Shrewsbury en-route from Hereford to Chester with an 11-coach train of preserved GWR coaches on 23 April 1977. *David Eatwell*

KING CLASS

GWR No	Name	Date Built	Double Chimney Fitted	Date Withdrawn	Shed Allocation 5/53	Shed Allocation 4/57	Final Shed	Notes
6000	King George V	6/27	12/56	12/62	Old Oak Common	Old Oak Common	Old Oak Common	1
6001	King Edward VII	7/27	2/56	9/62	Old Oak Common	Wolverhampton	Wolverhampton	
6002	King William IV	7/27	3/56	9/62	Old Oak Common	Old Oak Common	Wolverhampton	
6003	King George IV	7/27	4/57	6/62	Old Oak Common	Old Oak Common	Cardiff Canton	
6004	King George III	7/27	11/56	6/62	Wolverhampton	Laira	Cardiff Canton	
6005	King George II	7/27	7/56	11/62	Wolverhampton	Wolverhampton	Old Oak Common	
6006	King George I	2/28	6/56	2/62	Wolverhampton	Wolverhampton	Wolverhampton	
6007	King William III	3/28	9/56	9/62	Old Oak Common	Old Oak Common	Wolverhampton	2
6008	King James II	3/28	7/57	6/62	Laira	Laira	Wolverhampton	
6009	King Charles II	3/28	5/56	9/62	Old Oak Common	Old Oak Common	Old Oak Common	
6010	King Charles I	4/28	3/56	6/62	Laira	Laira	Cardiff Canton	
6011	King James I	4/28	3/56	12/62	Wolverhampton	Wolverhampton	Old Oak Common	
6012	King Edward VI	4/28	2/58	9/62	Laira	Old Oak Common	Wolverhampton	
6013	King Henry VIII	5/28	6/56	6/62	Old Oak Common	Old Oak Common	Wolverhampton	
6014	King Henry VII	5/28	9/57	9/62	Laira	Wolverhampton	Wolverhampton	3
6015	King Richard III	6/28	9/55	9/62	Old Oak Common	Old Oak Common	Wolverhampton	
6016	King Edward V	6/28	1/58	9/62	Wolverhampton	Old Oak Common	Wolverhampton	
6017	King Edward IV	6/28	12/55	7/62	Laira	Laira	Wolverhampton	
6018	King Henry VI	6/28	3/58	12/62	Old Oak Common	Old Oak Common	Old Oak Common	
6019	King Henry V	7/28	4/57	9/62	Old Oak Common	Old Oak Common	Old Oak Common	
6020	King Henry IV	5/30	8/56	7/62	Wolverhampton	Wolverhampton	Wolverhampton	
6021	King Richard II	6/30	3/57	9/62	Old Oak Common	Laira	Old Oak Common	
6022	King Edward III	6/30	5/56	9/62	Laira	Old Oak Common	Wolverhampton	
6023	King Edward II	6/30	6/57	6/62	Laira	Old Oak Common	Cardiff Canton	4
6024	King Edward I	6/30	3/57	6/62	Laira	Old Oak Common	Cardiff Canton	5
6025	King Henry III	7/30	3/57	12/62	Laira	Laira	Old Oak Common	
6026	King John	7/30	3/58	9/62	Laira	Laira	Old Oak Common	
6027	King Richard I	7/30	8/56	9/62	Laira	Laira	Wolverhampton	
6028	King George VI	7/30	1/57	11/62	Old Oak Common	Old Oak Common	Old Oak Common	6
6029	King Edward VIII	8/30	12/57	7/62	Laira	Laira	Old Oak Common	7

NOTES: All locomotives built at Swindon

1) Preserved as part of the National Collection and restored to running order by Messrs Bulmers Ltd, Hereford. The 6000 Locomotive Association are stewards to No 6000.
2) The original No 6007 was written-off in March 1936 after the Shrivenham accident and was replaced by a new locomotive.
3) Semi-streamlined in March 1935. Parts of this were removed in August 1935 and other parts by January 1943 with the exception of the wedged-shaped cab which was retained.
4) Purchased from Woodham Bros by Barry Steam Locomotive Action Group.
5) Rescued from Barry scrapyard by the 6024 Preservation Society Ltd and is undergoing restoration at Quainton Road.
6) Named *King Henry II* until January 1937.
7) Named *King Stephen* until May 1936.

'HALL' CLASS

No	Name	Date Built	Date Withdrawn	Notes
4900	Saint Martin	12/24	4/59	1
4901	Adderley Hall	12/28	9/60	
4902	Aldenham Hall	12/28	9/63	
4903	Astley Hall	12/28	10/64	
4904	Binnegar Hall	12/28	12/63	
4905	Barton Hall	12/28	11/63	
4906	Bradfield Hall	1/29	9/62	
4907	Broughton Hall	1/29	8/63	2
4908	Broome Hall	1/29	10/63	
4909	Blakesley Hall	1/29	9/62	
4910	Blaisdon Hall	1/29	12/63	
4911	Bowden Hall	2/29	6/41	3
4912	Berrington Hall	2/29	8/62	
4913	Baglan Hall	2/29	9/62	
4914	Cranmore Hall	2/29	12/63	
4915	Condover Hall	2/29	2/63	
4916	Crumlin Hall	2/29	8/64	
4917	Crosswood Hall	3/29	9/62	
4918	Dartington Hall	3/29	6/63	
4919	Donnington Hall	3/29	10/64	
4920	Dumbleton Hall	3/29	12/65	4
4921	Eaton Hall	4/29	9/62	
4922	Enville Hall	4/29	7/63	
4923	Evenley Hall	4/29	5/64	
4924	Eydon Hall	5/29	10/63	
4925	Eynsham Hall	5/29	8/62	
4926	Fairleigh Hall	5/29	9/61	
4927	Farnborough Hall	5/29	9/63	
4928	Gatacre Hall	5/29	12/63	
4929	Goytrey Hall	5/29	3/65	
4930	Hagley Hall	5/29	12/63	5
4931	Hanbury Hall	5/29	7/62	
4932	Hatherton Hall	6/29	11/64	
4933	Himley Hall	6/29	8/64	
4934	Hindlip Hall	6/29	9/62	
4935	Ketley Hall	6/29	3/63	
4936	Kinlet Hall	6/29	1/64	19
4937	Lanelay Hall	6/29	9/62	
4938	Liddington Hall	6/29	11/62	
4939	Littleton Hall	7/29	2/63	
4940	Ludford Hall	7/29	11/59	
4941	Llangedwyn Hall	7/29	10/62	
4942	Maindy Hall	7/29	12/63	6
4943	Marrington Hall	7/29	12/63	
4944	Middleton Hall	7/29	9/62	
4945	Milligan Hall	8/29	11/61	
4946	Moseley Hall	8/29	6/63	
4947	Nanhoran Hall	8/29	9/62	
4948	Northwick Hall	8/29	9/62	2
4949	Packwood Hall	8/29	9/64	
4950	Patshull Hall	8/29	5/64	
4951	Pendeford Hall	7/29	6/64	
4952	Peplow Hall	8/29	9/62	
4953	Pitchford Hall	8/29	5/63	
4954	Plaish Hall	8/29	11/64	
4955	Plaspower Hall	8/29	10/63	
4956	Plowden Hall	9/29	7/63	
4957	Postlip Hall	9/29	3/62	
4958	Priory Hall	9/29	9/64	
4959	Purley Hall	9/29	12/64	
4960	Pyle Hall	9/29	9/62	
4961	Pyrland Hall	11/29	11/62	
4962	Ragley Hall	11/29	10/65	
4963	Rignall Hall	11/29	6/62	
4964	Rodwell Hall	11/29	10/63	
4965	Rood Ashton Hall	11/29	3/62	
4966	Shakenhurst Hall	11/29	11/63	
4967	Shirenewton Hall	12/29	9/62	
4968	Shotton Hall	12/29	7/62	2
4969	Shrugborough Hall	12/29	9/62	
4970	Sketty Hall	12/29	7/63	
4971	Stanway Hall	1/30	8/62	2
4972	Saint Brides Hall	1/30	2/64	2
4973	Sweeney Hall	1/30	7/62	
4974	Talgarth Hall	1/30	4/62	
4975	Umberslade Hall	1/30	9/63	
4976	Warfield Hall	1/30	5/64	
4977	Watcombe Hall	1/30	5/62	
4978	Westwood Hall	2/30	9/64	
4979	Wootton Hall	2/30	12/63	
4980	Wrottesley Hall	2/30	7/63	
4981	Abberley Hall	12/30	10/63	
4982	Acton Hall	1/31	5/62	
4983	Albert Hall	1/31	12/63	7
4984	Albrighton Hall	1/31	9/62	
4985	Allesley Hall	1/31	9/64	
4986	Aston Hall	1/31	5/62	
4987	Brockley Hall	1/31	4/62	
4988	Bulwell Hall	1/31	2/64	
4989	Cherwell Hall	2/31	11/64	
4990	Clifton Hall	2/31	4/62	
4991	Cobham Hall	2/31	12/63	
4992	Crosby Hall	2/31	4/65	
4993	Dalton Hall	2/31	2/65	
4994	Downton Hall	2/31	3/63	
4995	Easton Hall	2/31	6/62	
4996	Eden Hall	3/31	9/63	
4997	Elton Hall	3/31	10/61	
4998	Eyton Hall	3/31	10/63	
4999	Gopsal Hall	3/31	9/62	
5900	Hinderton Hall	3/31	12/63	8
5901	Hazel Hall	5/31	6/64	
5902	Howick Hall	5/31	11/62	
5903	Keele Hall	5/31	9/63	
5904	Kelham Hall	5/31	11/63	
5905	Knowsley Hall	5/31	7/63	
5906	Lawton Hall	5/31	5/62	
5907	Marble Hall	5/31	11/61	
5908	Moreton Hall	6/31	7/63	
5909	Newton Hall	6/31	7/62	
5910	Park Hall	6/31	9/62	
5911	Preston Hall	6/31	9/62	
5912	Queen's Hall	6/31	12/62	
5913	Rushton Hall	6/31	5/62	
5914	Ripon Hall	7/31	1/64	
5915	Trentham Hall	7/31	1/60	
5916	Trinity Hall	7/31	7/62	
5917	Westminster Hall	7/31	9/62	
5918	Walton Hall	7/31	9/62	
5919	Worsley Hall	7/31	8/63	
5920	Wycliffe Hall	8/31	1/62	
5921	Bingley Hall	5/33	1/62	
5922	Caxton Hall	5/33	1/64	
5923	Colston Hall	5/33	12/63	
5924	Dinton Hall	5/33	12/63	
5925	Eastcote Hall	5/33	10/62	
5926	Grotrian Hall	6/33	9/62	
5927	Guild Hall	6/33	10/64	
5928	Haddon Hall	6/33	5/62	
5929	Hanham Hall	6/33	10/63	
5930	Hannington Hall	6/33	9/62	
5931	Hatherley Hall	6/33	9/62	
5932	Haydon Hall	6/33	10/65	
5933	Kingsway Hall	6/33	8/65	
5934	Kneller Hall	6/33	5/64	
5935	Norton Hall	7/33	5/62	
5936	Oakley Hall	7/33	1/65	
5937	Stanford Hall	7/33	11/63	
5938	Stanley Hall	7/33	5/63	
5939	Tangley Hall	7/33	10/64	
5940	Whitbourne Hall	8/33	9/62	
5941	Campion Hall	2/35	7/62	
5942	Doldowlod Hall	2/35	12/63	
5943	Elmdon Hall	3/35	6/63	
5944	Ickenham Hall	3/35	4/63	
5945	Leckhampton Hall	3/35	4/63	
5946	Marwell Hall	3/35	7/62	
5947	Saint Benet's Hall	3/35	7/62	
5948	Siddington Hall	3/35	8/63	
5949	Trematon Hall	4/35	5/61	
5950	Wardley Hall	4/35	11/61	
5951	Clyffe Hall	12/35	4/64	
5952	Cogan Hall	12/35	6/64	20
5953	Dunley Hall	12/35	10/62	
5954	Faendre Hall	12/35	10/63	
5955	Garth Hall	12/35	4/65	2
5956	Horsley Hall	12/35	3/63	
5957	Hutton Hall	12/35	7/64	
5958	Knolton Hall	1/36	3/64	
5959	Mawley Hall	1/36	9/62	
5960	Saint Edmund Hall	1/36	9/62	
5961	Toynbee Hall	6/36	8/65	
5962	Wantage Hall	7/36	11/64	
5963	Wimpole Hall	7/36	6/64	
5964	Wolseley Hall	7/36	9/62	
5965	Woollas Hall	8/36	7/62	
5966	Ashford Hall	3/37	9/62	
5967	Bickmarsh Hall	3/37	6/64	
5968	Cory Hall	3/37	9/62	
5969	Honington Hall	4/37	8/62	
5970	Hengrave Hall	4/37	11/63	
5971	Merevale Hall	4/37	12/65	
5972	Olton Hall	4/37	12/63	21
5973	Rolleston Hall	5/37	9/62	
5974	Wallsworth Hall	4/37	12/64	
5975	Winslow Hall	5/37	7/64	
5976	Ashwicke Hall	9/38	7/64	2
5977	Beckford Hall	9/38	8/63	

No	Name	Date Built	Date Withdrawn	Notes
5978	Bodinnick Hall	9/38	10/63	
5979	Cruckton Hall	9/38	11/64	
5980	Dingley Hall	9/38	9/62	
5981	Frensham Hall	10/38	9/62	
5982	Harrington Hall	10/38	9/62	
5983	Henley Hall	10/38	4/65	
5984	Linden Hall	10/38	1/65	
5985	Mostyn Hall	10/38	9/63	
5986	Arbury Hall	11/39	9/63	2
5987	Brocket Hall	11/39	1/64	
5988	Bostock Hall	11/39	10/65	
5989	Cransley Hall	12/39	7/62	
5990	Dorford Hall	12/39	1/65	
5991	Gresham Hall	12/39	7/64	
5992	Horton Hall	12/39	8/65	
5993	Kirby Hall	12/39	5/63	
5994	Roydon Hall	12/39	3/63	
5995	Wick Hall	1/40	4/63	
5996	Mytton Hall	6/40	8/62	
5997	Sparkford Hall	6/40	7/62	
5998	Trevor Hall	6/40	3/64	
5999	Wollaton Hall	6/40	9/62	
6900	Abney Hall	6/40	10/64	
6901	Arley Hall	7/40	6/64	
6902	Butlers Hall	7/40	5/61	
6903	Belmont Hall	7/40	9/65	
6904	Charfield Hall	7/40	1/65	
6905	Claughton Hall	7/40	6/64	
6906	Chicheley Hall	11/40	4/65	
6907	Davenham Hall	11/40	2/65	
6908	Downham Hall	11/40	7/65	
6909	Frewin Hall	11/40	6/64	
6910	Gossington Hall	12/40	10/65	
6911	Holker Hall	1/41	4/65	
6912	Helmster Hall	1/41	2/64	
6913	Levens Hall	2/41	6/64	
6914	Langton Hall	2/41	4/64	
6915	Mursley Hall	2/41	2/65	
6916	Misterton Hall	6/41	8/65	
6917	Oldlands Hall	6/41	9/65	
6918	Sandon Hall	6/41	9/65	
6919	Tylney Hall	6/41	8/63	
6920	Barningham Hall	7/41	12/63	
6921	Borwick Hall	7/41	10/65	
6922	Burton Hall	7/41	4/65	
6923	Croxteth Hall	7/41	12/65	
6924	Grantley Hall	8/41	10/65	
6925	Hackness Hall	8/41	11/64	
6926	Holkham Hall	11/41	5/65	
6927	Lilford Hall	11/41	10/65	
6928	Underley Hall	11/41	6/65	
6929	Whorlton Hall	11/41	10/63	
6930	Aldersey Hall	11/41	10/65	
6931	Aldborough Hall	12/41	10/65	
6932	Burwarton Hall	12/41	12/65	
6933	Birtles Hall	12/41	11/64	
6934	Beachamwell Hall	12/41	10/65	
6935	Browsholme Hall	12/41	2/65	
6936	Breccles Hall	7/42	11/64	
6937	Conyngham Hall	7/42	12/65	
6938	Corndean Hall	7/42	3/65	
6939	Calveley Hall	7/42	10/63	
6940	Didlington Hall	8/42	5/64	
6941	Fillongley Hall	8/42	4/64	
6942	Eshton Hall	8/42	12/64	
6943	Farnley Hall	8/42	12/63	
6944	Fledborough Hall	9/42	11/65	
6945	Glasfryn Hall	9/42	9/64	
6946	Heatherden Hall	12/42	6/64	
6947	Helmingham Hall	12/42	11/65	
6948	Holbrooke Hall	12/42	12/63	
6949	Haberfield Hall	12/42	5/61	2
6950	Kingsthorpe Hall	12/42	6/64	
6951	Impney Hall	2/43	12/65	
6952	Kimberley Hall	2/43	12/65	
6953	Leighton Hall	2/43	12/65	2
6954	Lotherton Hall	3/43	5/64	
6955	Lydcott Hall	3/43	2/65	
6956	Mottram Hall	3/43	12/65	
6957	Norcliffe Hall	4/43	10/65	2
6958	Oxburgh Hall	4/43	6/65	

'MODIFIED HALL' CLASS

No	Name	Date Built	Date Withdrawn	Notes
6959	Peatling Hall	3/44	12/65	
6960	Raveningham Hall	3/44	6/64	9
6961	Stedham Hall	3/44	9/65	
6962	Soughton Hall	4/44	1/63	
6963	Throwley Hall	4/44	7/65	
6964	Thornbridge Hall	5/44	9/65	
6965	Thirlestaine Hall	7/44	10/65	
6966	Witchingham Hall	5/44	9/64	
6967	Willesley Hall	8/44	12/65	
6968	Woodcock Hall	9/44	9/63	
6969	Wraysbury Hall	9/44	2/65	
6970	Whaddon Hall	9/44	6/64	
6971	Athelhampton Hall	10/47	10/64	
6972	Beningbrough Hall	10/47	3/64	
6973	Bricklehampton Hall	10/47	8/65	
6974	Bryngwyn Hall	10/47	5/65	
6975	Capesthorne Hall	10/47	12/63	
6976	Graythwaite Hall	10/47	10/65	
6977	Grundisburgh Hall	11/47	12/63	
6978	Haroldstone Hall	11/47	7/65	
6979	Helperly Hall	11/47	2/65	
6980	Llanrumney Hall	11/47	10/65	
6981	Marbury Hall	2/48	3/64	
6982	Melmerby Hall	1/48	8/64	
6983	Otterington Hall	2/48	8/65	
6984	Owsden Hall	2/48	12/65	
6985	Parwick Hall	2/48	9/64	
6986	Rydal Hall	3/48	4/65	
6987	Shervington Hall	3/48	9/64	
6988	Swithland Hall	3/48	9/64	
6989	Wightwick Hall	3/48	6/64	10
6990	Witherslack Hall	4/48	12/65	11
6991	Acton Burnell Hall	11/48	12/65	
6992	Arborfield Hall	11/48	6/64	
6993	Arthog Hall	12/48	12/65	
6994	Baggrave Hall	12/48	11/64	
6995	Benthall Hall	12/48	3/65	
6996	Blackwell Hall	1/49	10/64	
6997	Bryn-Ivor Hall	1/49	11/64	
6998	Burton Agnes Hall	1/49	12/65	12
6999	Capel Dewi Hall	2/49	12/65	
7900	Saint Peter's Hall	4/49	12/64	
7901	Dodington Hall	3/49	2/64	
7902	Eaton Mascot Hall	3/49	6/64	
7903	Foremarke Hall	4/49	6/64	22
7904	Fountains Hall	4/49	12/65	
7905	Fowey Hall	4/49	5/64	
7906	Fron Hall	12/49	3/65	
7907	Hart Hall	1/50	12/65	
7908	Henshall Hall	1/50	10/65	
7909	Heveningham Hall	1/50	11/65	
7910	Hown Hall	1/50	2/65	
7911	Lady Margaret Hall	2/50	12/63	
7912	Little Linford Hall	3/50	10/65	
7913	Little Wyrley Hall	3/50	3/65	
7914	Lleweni Hall	3/50	12/65	
7915	Mere Hall	3/50	10/65	
7916	Mobberley Hall	4/50	12/64	
7917	North Aston Hall	4/50	8/65	
7918	Rhose Wood Hall	4/50	2/65	
7919	Runter Hall	5/50	12/65	
7920	Coney Hall	9/50	6/65	
7921	Edstone Hall	9/50	12/63	
7922	Salford Hall	9/50	12/65	
7923	Speke Hall	9/50	6/65	
7924	Thornycroft Hall	9/50	12/65	
7925	Westol Hall	10/50	12/65	
7926	Willey Hall	10/50	12/64	
7927	Willington Hall	10/50	12/65	
7928	Wolf Hall	10/50	3/65	
7929	Wyke Hall	11/50	8/65	

'GRANGE' CLASS

No	Name	Date Built	Date Withdrawn	Notes
6800	Arlington Grange	8/36	6/64	
6801	Aylburton Grange	8/36	10/60	
6802	Bampton Grange	9/36	8/61	
6803	Bucklebury Grange	9/36	9/65	
6804	Brockington Grange	9/36	8/64	
6805	Broughton Grange	9/36	3/61	
6806	Blackwell Grange	9/36	10/64	
6807	Birchwood Grange	9/36	12/63	
6808	Beenham Grange	9/36	8/64	
6809	Burghclere Grange	9/36	7/63	
6810	Blakemere Grange	11/36	10/64	
6811	Cranbourne Grange	11/36	7/64	
6812	Chesford Grange	11/36	2/65	
6813	Eastbury Grange	12/36	9/65	
6814	Enborne Grange	12/36	12/63	
6815	Frilford Grange	12/36	11/65	

No	Name	Date Built	Date Withdrawn	Notes
816	Frankton Grange	12/36	7/65	
817	Gwenddwr Grange	12/36	4/65	
818	Hardwick Grange	12/36	4/64	
819	Highnam Grange	12/36	11/65	
820	Kingstone Grange	1/37	7/65	
821	Leaton Grange	1/37	11/64	
822	Manton Grange	1/37	9/64	
823	Oakley Grange	1/37	6/65	
824	Ashley Grange	1/37	4/64	
825	Llanvair Grange	2/37	6/64	
826	Nannerth Grange	2/37	5/65	
827	Llanfrechfa Grange	2/37	9/65	
828	Trellech Grange	2/37	7/63	
829	Burmington Grange	3/37	11/65	
830	Buckenhill Grange	8/37	10/65	
831	Bearley Grange	8/37	10/65	
832	Brockton Grange	8/37	1/64	
833	Calcot Grange	8/37	10/65	
834	Dummer Grange	8/37	6/64	
835	Eastham Grange	9/37	5/63	
836	Estevarney Grange	9/37	8/65	
837	Forthampton Grange	9/37	7/65	
838	Goodmoor Grange	9/37	11/65	
839	Hewell Grange	9/37	5/64	
840	Hazeley Grange	9/37	2/65	
841	Marlas Grange	9/37	6/65	
842	Nunhold Grange	9/37	11/64	
843	Poulton Grange	10/37	2/64	
844	Penhydd Grange	10/37	4/64	
845	Paviland Grange	10/37	9/64	
846	Ruckley Grange	10/37	9/64	
847	Tidmarsh Grange	10/37	12/65	
6848	Toddington Grange	10/37	12/65	
6849	Walton Grange	10/37	12/65	
6850	Cleeve Grange	10/37	12/64	
6851	Hurst Grange	11/37	8/65	
6852	Headbourne Grange	11/37	1/64	
6853	Morehampton Grange	11/37	10/65	
6854	Roundhill Grange	11/37	9/65	
6855	Saighton Grange	11/37	10/65	
6856	Stowe Grange	11/37	11/65	
6857	Tudor Grange	11/37	10/65	
6858	Woolston Grange	12/37	10/65	
6859	Yiewsley Grange	12/37	11/65	
6860	Aberporth Grange	2/39	2/65	
6861	Crynant Grange	2/39	10/65	
6862	Derwent Grange	2/39	6/65	
6863	Dolhywel Grange	2/39	11/64	
6864	Dymock Grange	2/39	10/65	
6865	Hopton Grange	3/39	5/62	
6866	Morfa Grange	3/39	5/65	
6867	Peterson Grange	3/39	8/64	
6868	Penrhos Grange	3/39	10/65	
6869	Resolven Grange	3/39	7/65	
6870	Bodicote Grange	3/39	9/65	
6871	Bourton Grange	3/39	10/65	
6872	Crawley Grange	3/39	12/65	
6873	Caradoc Grange	4/39	6/64	
6874	Haughton Grange	4/39	9/65	
6875	Hindford Grange	4/39	3/64	
6876	Kingsland Grange	4/39	11/65	
6877	Llanfair Grange	4/39	3/65	
6878	Longford Grange	5/39	11/64	
6879	Overton Grange	5/39	10/65	

'MANOR' CLASS

No	Name	Date Built	Date Withdrawn	Notes
7800	Torquay Manor	1/38	8/64	
7801	Anthony Manor	1/38	7/65	
7802	Bradley Manor	1/38	11/65	14
7803	Barcote Manor	1/38	4/65	
7804	Baydon Manor	2/38	9/65	
7805	Broome Manor	3/38	12/64	
7806	Cockington Manor	3/38	11/64	
7807	Compton Manor	3/38	11/64	
7808	Cookham Manor	3/38	12/65	13
7809	Childrey Manor	4/38	4/63	
7810	Draycott Manor	12/38	9/64	
7811	Dunley Manor	12/38	7/65	
7812	Erlestoke Manor	1/39	11/65	23
7813	Freshford Manor	1/39	5/65	
7814	Fringford Manor	1/39	9/65	
7815	Fritwell Manor	1/39	10/64	
7816	Frilsham Manor	1/39	11/65	
7817	Garsington Manor	1/39	6/64	
7818	Granville Manor	1/39	1/65	
7819	Hinton Manor	2/39	11/65	15
7820	Dinmore Manor	11/50	11/65	16
7821	Ditcheat Manor	11/50	11/65	20
7822	Foxcote Manor	12/50	11/65	17
7823	Hook Norton Manor	12/50	7/64	
7824	Iford Manor	12/50	11/64	
7825	Lechlade Manor	12/50	5/64	
7826	Longworth Manor	12/50	4/65	
7827	Lydham Manor	12/50	10/65	18
7828	Odney Manor	12/50	10/65	20
7829	Ramsbury Manor	12/50	12/65	

LOCOMOTIVES CONVERTED TO OIL BURNING

New No	Old No	Date Converted	Date Re-Converted		New No	Old No	Date Converted	Date Re-Converted
3900	4968	5/47	3/49		3952	6957	4/47	3/50
3901	4971	5/47	4/49		3953	6953	4/47	9/48
3902	4948	5/47	9/48		3954	5986	5/47	2/50
3903	4907	5/47	4/50		3955	6949	5/47	4/49
3904	4972	5/47	10/48					
3950	5955	6/46	10/48					
3951	5976	4/47	11/48					

No 5955 was renumbered in 10/46, the remainder when converted

NOTES FOR ALL CLASSES — All locomotives built at Swindon

1) Rebuilt from 'Saint' class and carried its old number 2925 until 12/28.
2) Converted to burn oil in 1946/7, see table above.
3) Received a direct hit from a German bomb at Keyham on 29 April 1941 and was condemned at Swindon on 10 June.
4) Rescued from Barry scrapyard by the Dumbleton Hall Preservation Society and is undergoing restoration on the Dart Valley Railway for use on the Torbay line.
5) Rescued from the Barry scrapyard and restored to main line running condition by the Severn Valley Railway.
6) Rescued from Barry scrapyard by the Great Western Society and awaits possible conversion to a 'Saint' class 4-6-0 at Didcot.
7) Rescued from Barry scrapyard by the Standard Gauge Steam Trust, Tyseley.
8) Rescued from Barry scrapyard by the Great Western Society and restored to main line running condition.
9) Rescued from Barry scrapyard and restored to main line running condition at Steamtown, Carnforth. Now on the Severn Valley Railway.
10) Rescued from Barry scrapyard by members of the Quainton Road Railway Society and undergoing restoration at Quainton Road.
11) Rescued from Barry scrapyard by the Witherslack Hall Society and is undergoing restoration at Loughborough.
12) Purchased from BR in running order by the Great Western Society.
13) Purchased from BR in running order by P. A. Lemar and is in the care of the Great Western Society at Didcot.
14) Rescued from Barry scrapyard by the Erlestoke Manor Fund and is undergoing restoration on the Severn Valley Railway.
15) Rescued from Barry scrapyard and restored to working order on the Severn Valley Railway.
16) Rescued from Barry scrapyard by the Gwili Railway Preservation Society and is undergoing restoration at Bronwydd Arms.
17) Rescued from Barry scrapyard by the Cambrian Railways Society Ltd and is undergoing restoration at Oswestry.
18) Rescued from Barry scrapyard and restored to working order on the Dart Valley Railway for use on the Torbay line.
19) Rescued from Barry scrapyard by the Peak Railway and is undergoing restoration at Buxton.
20) Rescued from Barry scrapyard by the Great Western Steam Locomotive Group and is undergoing restoration at Toddington.
21) Rescued from Barry scrapyard privately and is undergoing restoration at Wakefield.
22) Rescued from Barry scrapyard by Foremarke Hall Locomotive Group and is undergoing restoration at Blunsden.
23) Rescued from Barry scrapyard by Erlestoke Manor Fund and is now running on the Severn Valley Railway.

'COUNTY' CLASS

GWR No	Name	Date Built	Double Chimney Fitted	Date With-drawn	Shed Allocation 5/53	Shed Allocation 6/57	Final Shed	Notes
1000	County of Middlesex	8/45	3/58	7/64	Chester	Bristol Bath Rd	Swindon	1
1001	County of Bucks	9/45	12/57	5/63	Neyland	Neyland	Neyland	
1002	County of Berks	9/45	6/58	9/63	Laira	Penzance	Shrewsbury	
1003	County of Wilts	10/45	11/57	10/62	Penzance	Shrewsbury	Laira	
1004	County of Somerset	10/45	4/57	9/62	Wolverhampton	Swindon	Penzance	
1005	County of Devon	11/45	12/58	6/63	Bristol Bath Rd	Bristol Bath Rd	St Philip's Marsh	
1006	County of Cornwall	11/45	12/58	9/63	Laira	Penzance	Swindon	
1007	County of Brecknock	12/45	5/57	10/62	Bristol Bath Rd	Truro	Didcot	
1008	County of Cardigan	12/45	5/58	10/63	Chester	Chester	Swindon	
1009	County of Carmarthen	12/45	9/56	2/63	Neyland	Bristol Bath Rd	Swindon	
1010	County of Caernarvon	1/46	1/57	7/64	Laira	Laira	Swindon	2
1011	County of Chester	1/46	11/58	11/64	Bristol Bath Rd	Bristol Bath Rd	Swindon	
1012	County of Denbigh	2/46	9/57	4/64	Laira	Swindon	Swindon	
1013	County of Dorset	2/46	2/58	7/64	Shrewsbury	Shrewsbury	Swindon	
1014	County of Glamorgan	2/46	11/56	4/64	Bristol Bath Rd	Bristol Bath Rd	Swindon	
1015	County of Gloucester	3/46	11/58	11/62	Laira	Laira	Laira	
1016	County of Hants	3/46	3/57	9/63	Shrewsbury	Shrewsbury	Shrewsbury	
1017	County of Hereford	3/46	3/59	12/62	Shrewsbury	Shrewsbury	Shrewsbury	
1018	County of Leicester	3/46	1/58	9/62	Wolverhampton	Penzance	Didcot	
1019	County of Merioneth	4/46	3/59	2/63	Wolverhampton	Swindon	Shrewsbury	
1020	County of Monmouth	12/46	11/58	2/64	Neyland	Neyland	Swindon	
1021	County of Montgomery	12/46	10/59	11/63	Laira	Laira	St Philip's Marsh	
1022	County of Northampton	12/46	5/56	10/62	Chester	Chester	Shrewsbury	
1023	County of Oxford	1/47	5/57	3/63	Wolverhampton	Truro	Shrewsbury	
1024	County of Pembroke	1/47	7/58	4/64	Chester	Chester	Swindon	
1025	County of Radnor	1/47	8/59	2/63	Shrewsbury	Shrewsbury	Shrewsbury	
1026	County of Salop	1/47	10/58	9/62	Bristol Bath Rd	Shrewsbury	Shrewsbury	
1027	County of Stafford	3/47	8/56	10/63	Neyland	Neyland	Swindon	
1028	County of Warwick	3/47	8/58	12/63	Bristol Bath Rd	Bristol Bath Rd	Swindon	
1029	County of Worcester	4/47	5/59	12/62	Wolverhampton	Neyland	Swindon	

NOTES: All locomotives built at Swindon

1) Built with an experimental double chimney, later removed.
2) Name spelt Carnarvon until November 1951.

Publisher's Note
The information given in the tabular matter is correct to 1984.